Wild Animals at Home (annotated)

by Ernest Thompson Seton

Foreword

My travels in search of light on the "Animals at Home" have taken me up and down the Rocky Mountains for nearly thirty years. In the canyons from British Columbia to Mexico, I have lighted my campfire, far beyond the bounds of law and order, at times, and yet I have found no place more rewarding than the Yellowstone Park, the great mountain haven of wild life.

Whenever travellers penetrate into remote regions where human hunters are unknown, they find the wild things half tame, little afraid of man, and inclined to stare curiously from a distance of a few paces. But very soon they learn that man is their most dangerous enemy, and fly from him as soon as he is seen. It takes a long time and much restraint to win back their confidence.

In the early days of the West, when game abounded and when fifty yards was the extreme deadly range of the hunter's weapons, wild creatures were comparatively tame. The advent of the rifle and of the lawless skin hunter soon turned all big game into fugitives of excessive shyness and wariness. One glimpse of a man half a mile off, or a whiff of him on the breeze, was enough to make a Mountain Ram or a Wolf run for miles, though formerly these creatures would have gazed serenely from a point but a hundred yards removed.

The establishment of the Yellowstone Park in 1872 was the beginning of a new era of protection for wild life; and, by slow degrees, a different attitude in these animals toward us. In this Reservation, and nowhere else at present in the northwest, the wild things are not only abundant, but they have resumed their traditional Garden-of-Eden attitude toward man.

They come out in the daylight, they are harmless, and they are not afraid at one's approach. Truly this is ideal, a paradise for the naturalist and the camera hunter.

The region first won fame for its Canyon, its Cataracts and its Geysers, but I think its animal life has attracted more travellers than even the landscape beauties. I know it was solely the joy of being among the animals that led me to spend all one summer and part of another season in the Wonderland of the West.

My adventures in making these studies among the fourfoots have been very small adventures indeed; the thrillers are few and far between. Any one can go and have the same or better experiences to-day. But I give them as they happened, and if they furnish no ground for hair-lifting emotions, they will at least show what I was after and how I went.

I have aimed to show something of the little aspects of the creatures' lives, which are those that the ordinary traveller will see; I go with him indeed, pointing out my friends as they chance to pass, adding a few comments that should make for a better acquaintance on all sides. And I have offered glimpses, wherever possible, of the wild thing in its home, embodying in these chapters the substance of many lectures given under the same title as this book.

The cover design is by my wife, Grace Gallatin Seton. She was with me in most of the experiences narrated and had a larger share in every part of the work than might be inferred from the mere text.

ERNEST THOMPSON SETON.

Contents

I

The Cute Coyote

* * * * *

I

The Cute Coyote

AN EXEMPLARY LITTLE BEAST, MY FRIEND THE COYOTE

If you draw a line around the region that is, or was, known as the Wild West, you will find that you have exactly outlined the kingdom of the Coyote. He is even yet found in every part of it, but, unlike his big brother the Wolf, he never frequented the region known as Eastern America.

This is one of the few wild creatures that you can see from the train. Each time I have come to the Yellowstone Park I have discovered the swift gray form of the Coyote among the Prairie-dog towns along the River flat between Livingstone and Gardiner, and in the Park itself have seen him nearly every day, and heard him every night without exception.

Coyote (pronounced Ky-o'-tay, and in some regions Ky-ute) is a native Mexican contribution to the language, and is said to mean "halfbreed," possibly suggesting that the Coyote looks like a cross between the Fox and the Wolf. Such an origin would be a very satisfactory clue to his character, for he does seem to unite in himself every possible attribute in the mental make-up of the other two that can contribute to his success in life.

He is one of the few Park animals not now protected, for the excellent reasons, first that he is so well able to protect himself, second he is even already too numerous, third he is so destructive among the creatures that he can master. He is a beast of rare cunning; some of the Indians call him God's dog or Medicine dog. Some make him the embodiment of the Devil, and some going still further, in the light of their larger experience, make the Coyote the Creator himself seeking amusement in disguise among his creatures, just as did the Sultan in the "Arabian Nights."

The naturalist finds the Coyote interesting for other reasons. When you see that sleek gray and yellow form among the mounds of the Prairie-dog, at once creating a zone of blankness and silence by his very presence as he goes, remember that he is hunting for something to eat; also, that there is another, his mate, not far away. For the Coyote is an exemplary and moral little beast who has only one wife; he loves her devotedly, and they fight the life battle together. Not only is there sure to be a mate close by, but that mate, if invisible, is likely to be playing a game, a very clever game as I have seen it played.

Furthermore, remember there is a squealing brood of little Coyotes in the home den up on a hillside a mile or two away. Father and mother must hunt continually and successfully to furnish their daily food. The dog-towns are their game preserves, but how are they to catch a Prairie-dog! Every one knows that though these little yapping Ground-squirrels will sit up and bark at an express train but twenty feet away, they scuttle down out of sight the moment a man, dog or Coyote enters into the far distant precincts of their town; and downstairs they stay in the cyclone cellar until after a long interval of quiet that probably proves the storm to be past. Then they poke their prominent eyes above the level, and, if all is still, will softly hop out and in due course, resume their feeding.

THE PRAIRIE-DOG OUTWITTED

This is how the clever Coyote utilizes these habits. He and his wife approach the dog-town unseen. One Coyote hides, then the other walks forward openly into the town. There is a great barking of all the Prairie-dogs as they see their enemy approach, but they dive down when he is amongst them. As soon as they are out of sight the second Coyote rushes forward and hides near any promising hole that happens to have some sort of cover close by. Meanwhile, Coyote number one strolls on. The Prairie-dogs that he scared below come up again. At first each puts up the top of his head merely, with his eyes on bumps, much like those of a hippopotamus, prominent and peculiarly suited for this observation work from below, as they are the first things above ground. After a brief inspection, if all be quiet, he comes out an inch more. Now he can look around, the coast is clear, so he sits up on the mound and scans his surroundings.

Yes! Ho! Ho! he sees his enemy, that hated Coyote, strolling away off beyond the possibility of doing harm. His confidence is fully restored as the Coyote gets smaller in the distance and the other Prairie-dogs coming out seem to endorse his decision and give him renewed confidence. After one or two false starts, he sets off to feed. This means go ten or twenty feet from the door of his den, for all the grass is eaten off near home.

Among the herbage he sits up high to take a final look around, then burying his nose in the fodder, he begins his meal. This is the chance that the waiting, watching, she-Coyote counted on. There is a flash of gray fur from behind that little grease bush; in three hops she is upon him. He takes alarm at the first sound and tries to reach the haven hole, but she snaps him up. With a shake she ends his troubles. He hardly knows the pain of death, then she bounds away on her back track to the home den on the distant hillside. She does not come near it openly and rashly. There is always the possibility of such an approach betraying the family to some strong enemy on watch. She circles around a little, scrutinizes the landscape, studies the tracks and the wind, then comes to the door by more or less devious hidden ways. The sound of a foot outside is enough to make the little ones cower in absolute silence, but mother reassures them with a whining call much like that of a dog mother. They rush out, tumbling over each other in their glee, six or seven in number usually, but sometimes as high as ten or twelve. Eagerly they come, and that fat Prairie-dog lasts perhaps three minutes, at the end of which time nothing is left but the larger bones with a little Coyote busy polishing each of them. Strewn about the door of the den are many other kindred souvenirs, the bones of Ground-squirrels, Chipmunks, Rabbits, Grouse, Sheep, and Fawns, with many kinds of feathers, fur, and hair, to show the great diversity of Coyote diet.

THE COYOTE'S SENSE OF HUMOUR

To understand the Coyote fully one must remember that he is simply a wild dog, getting his living by his wits, and saving his life by the tireless serviceability of his legs; so has developed both these gifts to an admirable pitch of perfection. He is blessed further with a gift of music and a sense of humour.

When I lived at Yancey's, on the Yellowstone, in 1897, I had a good example of the latter, and had it daily for a time. The dog attached to the camp on the inner circle was a conceited, irrepressible little puppy named Chink. He was so full of energy, enthusiasm, and courage that there was no room left in him for dog-sense. But it came after a vast number of humiliating experiences.

A Coyote also had attached himself to the camp, but on the outer circle. At first he came out by night to feed on the garbage pile, but realizing the peace of the Park he became bolder and called occasionally by day. Later he was there every day, and was often seen sitting on a ridge a couple of hundred yards away.

One day he was sitting much nearer and grinning in Coyote fashion, when one of the campers in a spirit of mischief said to the dog, "Chink, you see that Coyote out there grinning at you. Go and chase him out of that."

Burning to distinguish himself, that pup set off at full speed, and every time he struck the ground he let off a war-whoop. Away went the Coyote and it looked like a good race to us, and to the Picket-pin Ground-squirrels that sat up high on their mounds to rejoice in the spectacle of these, their enemies, warring against each other.

The Coyote has a way of slouching along, his tail dangling and tangling with his legs, and his legs loose-jointed, mixing with his tail. He doesn't seem to work hard but oh! how he does cover the prairie! And very soon it was clear that in spite of his magnificent bounds and whoops of glory, Chink was losing ground. A little later the Coyote obviously had to slack up to keep from running away altogether. It had seemed a good race for a quarter of a mile, but it was nothing to the race which began when the Coyote turned on Chink. Uttering a gurgling growl, a bark, and a couple of screeches, he closed in with all the combined fury of conscious might and right, pitted against unfair unprovoked attack.

And Chink had a rude awakening; his war-whoops gave place to yelps of dire distress, as he wheeled and made for home. But the Coyote could run all around him, and nipped him, here and there, and when he would, and seemed to be cracking a series of good jokes at Chink's expense, nor ever stopped till the ambitious one of boundless indiscretion was hidden under his master's bed.

This seemed very funny at the time, and I am afraid Chink did not get the sympathy he was entitled to, for after all he was merely carrying out orders. But he made up his mind that from that time on, orders or no orders, he would let Coyotes very much alone. They were not so easy as they looked.

The Coyote, however, had discovered a new amusement. From that day he simply "laid" for that little dog, and if he found him a hundred yards or so from camp, would chase and race him back in terror to some shelter. At last things got so bad that if we went for a ride even, and Chink followed us, the Coyote would come along, too, and continue his usual amusement.

At first it was funny, and then it became tedious, and at last it was deeply resented by Chink's master. A man feels for his dog; he wasn't going to stand still and see his dog abused. He began to grumble vaguely about "If something didn't happen pretty soon, something else would." Just what he meant I didn't ask, but I know that the Coyote disappeared one day, and never was seen or heard of again. I'm not supposed to know any thing about it, but I have my suspicions, although in those days the Coyote was a protected animal.

HIS DISTINGUISHING GIFT

The scientific name of the Coyote (Canis latrans), literally "Barking Dog," is given for the wonderful yapping chorus with which they seldom fail to announce their presence in the evening, as they gather at a safe distance from the campfire. Those not accustomed to the sound are very ready to think that they are surrounded by a great pack of ravening Wolves, and get a sufficiently satisfactory thrill of mingled emotions at the sound. But the guide will reassure you by saying that that great pack of howling Wolves is nothing more than a harmless little Coyote, perhaps two, singing their customary vesper song, demonstrating their wonderful vocal powers. Their usual music begins with a few growling, gurgling yaps which are rapidly increased in volume and heightened in pitch, until they rise into a long squall or scream, which again, as it dies away, breaks up into a succession of yaps and gurgles. Usually one Coyote begins it, and the others join in with something like agreement on the scream.

I believe I never yet camped in the West without hearing this from the near hills when night time had come. Last September I even heard it back of the Mammoth Hot Springs Hotel, and I must say I have learned to love it. It is a wild, thrilling, beautiful song. Our first camp was at Yancey's last summer and just after we had all turned in, the Coyote chorus began, a couple of hundred yards from the camp. My wife sat up and exclaimed, "Isn't it glorious? now I know we are truly back in the West."

The Park authorities are making great efforts to reduce the number of Coyotes because of their destructiveness to the young game, but an animal that is endowed with extraordinary wits, phenomenal speed, unexcelled hardihood, and marvellous fecundity, is not easily downed. I must confess that if by any means they should succeed in exterminating the Coyote in the West, I should feel that I had lost something of very great value. I never fail to get that joyful thrill when the "Medicine Dogs" sing their "Medicine Song" in the dusk, or the equally weird and thrilling chorus with which they greet the dawn; for they have a large repertoire and a remarkable register. The Coyote is indeed the Patti of the Plains.

THE COYOTE'S SONG[A]

I am the Coyote that sings each night at dark; It was by gobbling prairie-dogs that I got such a bark. At least a thousand prairie-dogs I fattened on, you see, And every bark they had in them is reproduced in me.

Refrain:

I can sing to thrill your soul or pierce it like a lance, And all I ask of you to do is give me half a chance. With a yap--yap--yap for the morning And a yoop--yoop--yoop for the night And a yow--wow--wow for the rising moon And a yah-h-h-h for the campfire light. Yap--yoop--yow--yahhh!

I gathered from the howling winds, the frogs and crickets too, And so from each availing fount, my inspiration drew. I warbled till the little birds would quit their native bush. And squat around me on the ground in reverential hush.

Refrain:

I'm a baritone, soprano, and a bass and tenor, too. I can thrill and slur and frill and whirr and shake you through and through. I'm a Jews' harp--I'm an organ--I'm a fiddle and a flute. Every kind of touching sound is found in the coyoot.

Refrain:

I'm a whooping howling wilderness, a sort of Malibran. With Lind, Labache and Melba mixed and all combined in one. I'm a grand cathedral organ and a calliope sharp, I'm a gushing, trembling nightingale, a vast aeolian harp.

Refrain:

I can raise the dead or paint the town, or pierce you like a lance And all I ask of you to do is to give me half a chance. Etc., etc., etc.

(Encore verses)

Although I am a miracle, I'm not yet recognized. Oh, when the world does waken up how highly I'll be prized. Then managers and vocal stars--and emperors effete Shall fling their crowns, their money bags, their persons, at my feet.

Refrain:

I'm the voice of all the Wildest West, the Patti of the Plains; I'm a wild Wagnerian opera of diabolic strains; I'm a roaring, ranting orchestra with lunatics be-crammed; I'm a vocalized tornado--I'm the shrieking of the damned.

Refrain:

[Illustration]

FOOTNOTES:

* * * * *

II

The Prairie-dog and His Kin

* * * * *

II

The Prairie-dog and His Kin

MERRY YEK-YEK AND HIS LIFE OF TROUBLES

The common Prairie-dog is typical of the West, more so than the Buffalo is, and its numbers, even now, rival those of the Buffalo in its palmiest days. I never feel that I am truly back on the open range till I hear their call and see the Prairie-dogs once more upon their mounds. As you travel up the Yellowstone Valley from Livingstone to Gardiner you may note in abundance this "dunce of the plains." The "dog-towns" are frequent along the railway, and at each of the many burrows you see from one to six of the inmates. As you come near Gardiner there is a steady rise of the country, and somewhere near the edge of the Park the elevation is such that it imposes one of those mysterious barriers to animal extension which seem to be as impassable as they are invisible. The Prairie-dog range ends near the Park gates. General George S. Anderson tells me, however, that individuals are occasionally found on the flats along the Gardiner River, but always near the gate, and never elsewhere in the Park. On this basis, then, the Prairie-dog is entered as a Park animal.

It is, of course, a kind of Ground-squirrel. The absurd name "dog" having been given on account of its "bark." This call is a high-pitched "yek-yek-yek-yeeh," uttered as an alarm cry while the creature sits up on the mound by its den, and every time it "yeks" it jerks up its tail. Old timers will tell you that the Prairie-dog's voice is tied to its tail, and prove it by pointing out that one is never raised without the other.

As we have seen, the Coyote looks on the dog-town much as a cow does on a field of turnips or alfalfa--a very proper place, to seek for wholesome, if commonplace, sustenance. But Coyotes are not the only troubles in the life of Yek-yek.

Ancient books and interesting guides will regale the traveller with most acceptable stories about the Prairie-dog, Rattlesnake, and the Burrowing Owl, all living in the same den on a basis of brotherly love and Christian charity; having effected, it would seem, a limited partnership and a most satisfactory division of labour: the Prairie-dog is to dig the hole, the Owl to mount sentry and give warning of all danger, and the Rattler is to be ready to die at his post as defender of the Prairie-dog's young. This is pleasing if true.

There can be no doubt that at times all three live in the same burrow, and in dens that the hard-working rodent first made. But the simple fact is that the Owl and the Snake merely use the holes abandoned (perhaps under pressure) by the Prairie-dog; and if any two of the three underground worthies happen to meet in the same hole, the fittest survives. I suspect further that the young of each kind are fair game and acceptable, dainty diet to each of the other two.

Farmers consider Prairie-dogs a great nuisance; the damage they do to crops is estimated at millions per annum. The best way to get rid of them, practically the only way, is by putting poison down each and every hole in the town, which medieval Italian mode has become the accepted method in the West.

Poor helpless little Yek-yek, he has no friends; his enemies and his list of burdens increase. The prey of everything that preys, he yet seems incapable of any measure of retaliation. The only visible joy in his life is his daily hasty meal of unsucculent grass, gathered between cautious looks around for any new approaching trouble, and broken by so many dodges down the narrow hole that his ears are worn off close to his head. Could any simpler, smaller pleasure than his be discovered? Yet he is fat and merry; undoubtedly he enjoys his every day on earth, and is as unwilling as any of us to end the tale. We can explain him only if we credit him with a philosophic power to discover happiness within in spite of all the cold unfriendly world about him.

THE WHISTLER IN THE ROCKS

When the far-off squirrel ancestor of Yek-yek took to the plains for a range, another of the family selected the rocky hills.

He developed bigger claws for the harder digging, redder colour for the red-orange surroundings, and a far louder and longer cry for signalling across the peaks and canyons, and so became the bigger, handsomer, more important creature we call the Mountain Whistler, Yellow Marmot or Orange Woodchuck.

In all of the rugged mountain parts of the Yellowstone one may hear his peculiar, shrill whistle, especially in the warm mornings.

You carefully locate the direction of the note and proceed to climb toward it. You may have an hour's hard work before you sight the orange-breasted Whistler among the tumbled mass of rocks that surround his home, for it is a far-reaching sound, heard half a mile away at times.

Those who know the Groundhog of the East would recognize in the Rock Woodchuck its Western cousin, a little bigger, yellower, and brighter in its colours, living in the rocks and blessed with a whistle that would fill a small boy with envy. Now, lest the critical should object to the combination name of "Rock Woodchuck," it is well to remind them that "Woodchuck" has nothing to do with either "wood" or "chucking," but is our corrupted form of an Indian name "Ot-choeck," which is sometimes written also "We-jack."

In the ridge of broken rocks just back of Yancey's is a colony of the Whistlers; and there as I sat sketching one day, with my camera at hand, one poked his head up near me and gave me the pose that is seen in the photograph.

THE PACK-RAT AND HIS MUSEUM

Among my school fellows was a boy named Waddy who had a mania for collecting odds, ends, curios, bits of brass or china, shiny things, pebbles, fungus, old prints, bones, business cards, carved peach stones, twisted roots, distorted marbles, or freak buttons. Anything odd or glittering was his especial joy. He had no theory about these things. He did not do anything in particular with them. He found gratification in spreading them out to gloat over, but I think his chief joy was in the collecting. And when some comrade was found possessed of a novelty that stirred his cupidity, the pleasure of planning a campaign to secure possession, the working out of the details, and the glory of success, were more to Waddy than any other form of riches or exploit.

The Pack-rat is the Waddy of the mountains, or Waddy was the Pack-rat of the school. Imagine, if you would picture the Pack-rat, a small creature like a common rat, but with soft fur, a bushy tail, and soulful eyes, living the life of an ordinary rat in the woods, except that it has an extraordinary mania for collecting curios.

There can be little doubt that this began in the nest-building idea, and then, because it was necessary to protect his home, cactus leaves and thorny branches were piled on it. The instinct grew until to-day the nest of a Pack-rat is a mass of rubbish from one to four feet high, and four to eight feet across. I have examined many of these collections. They are usually around the trunks in a clump of low trees, and consist of a small central nest about eight inches across, warm and soft, with a great mass of sticks and thorns around and over this, leaving a narrow entrance well-guarded by an array of cactus spines; then on top of all, a most wonderful collection of pine cones, shells, pebbles, bones, scraps of paper and tin, and the skulls of other animals. And when the owner can add to these works of art or vertu a brass cartridge, a buckle or a copper rivet, his little bosom is doubtless filled with the same high joy that any great collector might feel on securing a Raphael or a Rembrandt.

I remember finding an old pipe in one Rat museum. Pistol cartridges are eagerly sought after, so are saddle buckles, even if he has to cut them surreptitiously from the saddle of some camper. And when any of these articles are found missing it is usual to seek out the nearest Rat house, and here commonly the stolen goods are discovered shamelessly exposed on top. I remember hearing of a set of false teeth that were lost in camp, but rescued in this very way.

A FREE TRADER

"Pack" is a Western word meaning "carry," and thus the Rat that carries off things is the "Pack-rat." But it has another peculiarity. As though it had a conscience disturbed by pilfering the treasure of another, it often brings back what may be considered a fair exchange. Thus a silver-plated spoon may have gone from its associate cup one night, but in that cup you may find a long pine cone or a surplus nail, by which token you may know that a Pack-rat has called and collected. Sometimes this enthusiastic fancier goes off with food, but leaves something in its place; in one case that I heard of, the Rat, either with a sense of humour or a mistaken idea of food values, after having carried off the camp biscuit, had filled the vacant dish with the round pellets known as "Elk sign." But evidently there is a disposition to deal fair; not to steal, but to trade. For this reason the creature is widely known as the "Trade Rat."

Although I have known the Pack-rat for years in the mountains, I never saw one within the strict lines of the Yellowstone sanctuary. But the guides all assure me that they are found and manifest the same disposition here as elsewhere. So that if you should lose sundry bright things around camp, or some morning find your boots stuffed with pebbles, deer sign, or thorns, do not turn peevish or charge the guide with folly; it means, simply, you have been visited by a Mountain Rat, and any uneatables you miss will doubtless be found in his museum, which will be discovered within a hundred yards--a mass of sticks and rubbish under a tree--with some bright and shiny things on the top where the owner can sit amongst them on sunny days, and gloat till his little black eyes are a-swim, and his small heart filled with holy joy.

THE UPHEAVER--THE MOLE-GOPHER

As you cross any of the level, well-grassed prairie regions in the Yellowstone you will see piles of soft earth thrown up in little hillocks, sometimes a score or more of them bunched together. The drivers will tell you that these are molehills, which isn't quite true. For the Mole is a creature unknown in the Park, and the animal that makes these mounds is exceedingly abundant. It is the common Mole-gopher, a gopher related very distantly to the Prairie-dog and Mountain Whistler, but living the underground life of a Mole, though not even in the same order as that interesting miner, for the Mole-gopher is a rodent (Order Rodentia) and the Mole a bug-eater (Order Insectivora); just as different as Lion and Caribou.

The Mole-gopher is about the size of a rat, but has a short tail and relatively immense forepaws and claws. It is indeed wonderfully developed as a digger.

Examine the mound of earth thrown up. If it is a fair example, it will make fully half a bushel. Next count the mounds that are within a radius of fifty paces; probably all are the work of this Gopher, or rather this pair, for they believe in team play.

Search over the ground carefully, and you will discern that there are scores of ancient mounds flattened by the weather, and traces of hundreds, perhaps, that date from remote years.

Now multiply the size of one mound by the number of mounds, and you will have some idea of the work done by this pair. Finally, remembering that there may be a pair of Gophers for every acre in the Park, estimate the tons of earth moved by one pair and multiply it by the acres in the Park, and you will get an idea of the work done by those energetic rodents as a body, and you will realize how well he has won his Indian name, the "Upheaver."

We are accustomed to talk of upheaval in geology as a frightful upset of all nature, but here before our eyes is going on an upheaval of enormous extent and importance, but so gently and pleasantly done that we enjoy every phase of the process.

* * * * *

III

Famous Fur-bearers--

* * * * *

III

Famous Fur-bearers

FOX, MARTEN, BEAVER, AND OTTER

Fair Lady Multo Millionaire riding in the dusty stagecoach, comparing as you go the canyons of the Yellowstone with memories of Colorado, Overland, and Stalheim, you, in your winter home, know all about fur as it enters your world with its beauty, its warmth, its price--its gauge of the wearer's pocket. Let me add a segment of the circle to round your knowledge out.

When nature peopled with our four-foot kin the cold north lands, it was necessary to clothe these little brethren of ours in a coat that should be absolutely warm, light, durable, of protective colour, thick in cold weather, thin in warm. Under these conditions she produced fur, with its densely woolly undercoat and its long, soft, shining outer coat, one for warmth, the other for wet and wear. Some northern animals can store up food in holes or in the fat of their bodies, so need not be out when the intensest cold is on the land. Some have to face the weather all winter, and in these we find the fur of its best quality. Of this class are the Marten and the Northern Fox. They are the finest, warmest, lightest, softest of all furs. But colour is a cardinal point when beauty is considered and where fashion is Queen. So the choicest colours are the soft olive brown with silver hairs, found in the Russian Sable, and the glossy black with silver hairs, found in the true Silver Fox of the North.

THE MOST WONDERFUL FUR IN THE WORLD

What is the Silver Fox? Simply a black freak, a brunette born into a red-headed family. But this does not cast any reflection on the mother or on father's lineage. On the contrary, it means that they had in them an element of exceptional vigour, which resulted in a peculiar intensifying of all pigments, transmuting red into black and carrying with it an unusual vigour of growth and fineness of texture, producing, in short, the world-famed Silver Fox, the lightest, softest, thickest, warmest, and most lustrous of furs, the fur worth many times its weight in gold, and with this single fault, that it does not stand long wear.

Cold and exposure are wonderful stimulants of the skin, and so it is not surprising that the real Silver Fox should appear only in very cold climates. Owing to its elevation the Yellowstone Park has the winter climate of northern Canada, and, as might have been predicted, the Silver Fox occurs among the many red-headed or bleached blonde Foxes that abound in the half open country.

You may travel all round the stage route and neither see nor hear a Fox, but travel quietly on foot, or better, camp out, and you will soon discover the crafty one in yellow, or, rather, he will discover you. How? Usually after you have camped for the night and are sitting quietly by the fire before the hour of sleep, a curious squall is heard from the dark hillside or bushes, a squall followed by a bark like that of a toy terrier. Sometimes it keeps on at intervals for five minutes, and sometimes it is answered by a similar noise. This is the bark of a Fox. It differs from the Coyote call in being very short, very squally, much higher pitched, and without any barks in it that would do credit to a fair-sized dog. It is no use to go after him. You won't see him. You should rather sit and enjoy the truly wildwood ring of his music.

In the morning if you look hard in the dust and mud, you may find his tracks, and once in a while you will see his yellow-brown form drifting on the prairie as though wind-blown under sail of that enormous tail. For this is the big-tailed variety of Red Fox.

But if you wish to see the Fox in all his glory you must be here in winter, when the deep snow cutting off all other foods brings all the Fox population about the hotels whose winter keepers daily throw out scraps for which the Foxes, the Magpies, and a dozen other creatures wait and fight.

From a friend, connected with one of the Park hotels during the early '90's, I learned that among the big-tailed pensioners of the inn, there appeared one winter a wonderful Silver Fox; and I heard many rumours about that Fox. I was told that he disappeared, and did not die of sickness, old age, or wild-beast violence; and what I heard I may tell in a different form, only, be it remembered, the names of the persons and places are disguised, as well as the date; and my informant may have brought in details that belonged elsewhere. So that you are free to question much of the account, but the backbone of it is not open to doubt, and some of the guides in the Park can give you details that I do not care to put on paper.

THE POACHER AND THE SILVER FOX

How is it that all mankind has a sneaking sympathy with a poacher? A burglar or a pickpocket has our unmitigated contempt; he clearly is a criminal;

but you will notice that the poacher in the story is generally a reckless dare-devil with a large and compensatory amount of good-fellow in his make-up--yes, I almost said, of good citizenship. I suppose, because in addition to the breezy, romantic character of his calling, seasoned with physical danger as well as moral risk, there is away down in human nature a strong feeling that, in spite of man-made laws, the ancient ruling holds that "wild game belongs to no man till some one makes it his property by capture." It may be wrong, it may be right, but I have heard this doctrine voiced by red men and white, as primitive law, once or twice; and have seen it lived up to a thousand times.

Well, Josh Cree was a poacher. This does not mean that every night in every month he went forth with nefarious tricks and tools, to steal the flesh and fur that legally were not his. Far from it. Josh never poached but once. But that's enough; he had crossed the line, and this is how it came about:

As you roll up the Yellowstone from Livingston to Gardiner you may note a little ranch-house on the west of the track with its log stables, its corral, its irrigation ditch, and its alfalfa patch of morbid green. It is a small affair, for it was founded by the handiwork of one honest man, who with his wife and small boy left Pennsylvania, braved every danger of the plains, and secured this claim in the late '80's. Old man Cree--he was only forty, but every married man is "Old Man" in the West--was ready to work at any honest calling from logging or sluicing to grading and muling. He was strong and steady, his wife was steady and strong. They saved their money, and little by little they got the small ranch-house built and equipped; little by little they added to their stock on the range with the cattle of a neighbour, until there came the happy day when they went to live on their own ranch--father, mother, and fourteen-year-old Josh, with every prospect of making it pay. The spreading of that white tablecloth for the first time was a real religious ceremony, and the hard workers gave thanks to the All-father for His blessing on their every effort.

One year afterward a new event brought joy; there entered happily into their happy house a little girl, and all the prairie smiled about them. Surely their boat was well beyond the breakers.

But right in the sunshine of their joy the trouble cloud arose to block the sky. Old man Cree was missing one day. His son rode long and far on the range for two hard days before he sighted a grazing pony, and down a rocky hollow near, found his father, battered and weak, near death, with a broken leg and a gash in his head.

He could only gasp "Water" as Josh hurried up, and the boy rushed off to fill his hat at the nearest stream.

They had no talk, for the father swooned after drinking, and Josh had to face the situation; but he was Western trained. He stripped himself of all spare clothing, and his father's horse of its saddle blanket; then, straightening out the sick man, he wrapped him in the clothes and blanket, and rode like mad for the nearest ranch-house. The neighbour, a young man, came at once, with a pot to make tea, an axe, and a rope. They found the older Cree conscious but despairing. A fire was made, and hot tea revived him. Then Josh cut two long poles from the nearest timber and made a stretcher, or travois, Indian fashion, the upper ends fast to the saddle of a horse, while the other ends trailed on the ground. Thus by a long, slow journey the wounded man got back. All he had prayed for was to get home. Every invalid is sure that if only he can get home all will soon be well. Mother was not yet strong, the baby needed much care, but Josh was a good boy, and the loving best of all was done for the sick one. His leg, set by the army surgeon of Fort Yellowstone, was knit again after a month, but had no power. He had no force; the shock of those two dire days was on him. The second month went by, and still he lay in bed. Poor Josh was the man of the place now, and between duties, indoors and out, he was worn body and soul.

Then it was clear they must have help. So Jack S---- was engaged at the regular wages of $40 a month for outside work, and a year of struggle went by, only to see John Cree in his grave, his cattle nearly all gone, his widow and boy living in a house on which was still $500 of the original mortgage. Josh was a brave boy and growing strong, but unboyishly grave with the weight of care. He sold off the few cattle that were left, and set about keeping the roof over his mother and baby sister by working a truck farm for the market supplied by the summer hotels of the Park, and managed to come out even. He would in time have done well, but he could not get far enough ahead to meet that 10 per cent mortgage already overdue.

The banker was not a hard man, but he was in the business for the business.

He extended the time, and waited for interest again and again, but it only made the principal larger, and it seemed that the last ditch was reached, that it would be best to let the money-man foreclose, though that must mean a wipe-out and would leave the fatherless family homeless.

Winter was coming on, work was scarce, and Josh went to Gardiner to see what he could get in the way of house or wage. He learned of a chance to 'substitute' for the Park mail-carrier, who had sprained his foot. It was an easy drive to Fort Yellowstone, and there he readily agreed, when they asked him, to take the letters and packages and go on farther to the Canyon Hotel. Thus it was that on the 20th day of November 189--, Josh Cree, sixteen years old, tall and ruddy, rode through the snow to the kitchen door of the Canyon Hotel and was welcomed as though he were old Santa Claus himself.

Two Magpies on a tree were among the onlookers. The Park Bears were denned up, but there were other fur-bearers about. High on the wood-pile sat a Yellow Red Fox in a magnificent coat. Another was in front of the house, and the keeper said that as many as a dozen came some days. And sometimes, he said, there also came a wonderful Silver Fox, a size bigger than the rest, black as coal, with eyes like yellow diamonds, and a silver frosting like little stars on his midnight fur.

"My! but he's a beauty. That skin would buy the best team of mules on the Yellowstone." That was interesting and furnished talk for a while. In the morning when they were rising for their candlelight breakfast, the hotel man glancing from the window exclaimed, "Here he is now!" and Josh peered forth to see in the light of sunrise something he had often heard of, but never before seen, a coal-black Fox, a giant among his kind. How slick and elegant his glossy fur, how slim his legs, and what a monstrous bushy tail; and the other Foxes moved aside as the patrician rushed in impatient haste to seize the food thrown out by the cook.

"Ain't he a beauty?" said the hotel man. "I'll bet that pelt would fetch five hundred."

Oh, why did he say "five hundred," the exact sum, for then it was that the tempter entered into Josh Cree's heart. Five hundred dollars! just the amount of the mortgage. "Who owns wild beasts? The man that kills them," said the tempter, and the thought was a live one in his breast as Josh rode back to Fort Yellowstone.

At Gardiner he received his pay, $6, for three days' work and, turning it into groceries, set out for the poor home that soon would be lost to him, and as he rode he did some hard and gloomy thinking. On his wrist there hung a wonderful Indian quirt of plaited rawhide and horsehair with beads on the shaft, and a band of Elk teeth on the butt. It was a pet of his, and "good medicine," for a flat piece of elkhorn let in the middle was perforated with a hole, through which the distant landscape was seen much clearer--a well-known law, an ancient trick, but it made the quirt prized as a thing of rare virtue, and Josh had refused good offers for it. Then a figure afoot was seen, and coming nearer, it turned out to be a friend, Jack Day, out a-gunning with a .22 rifle. But game was scarce and Jack was returning to Gardiner empty-handed and disgusted. They stopped for a moment's greeting when Day said: "Huntin's played out now. How'll you swap that quirt for my rifle?" A month before Josh would have scorned the offer. A ten-dollar quirt for a five-dollar rifle, but now he said briefly: "For rifle with cover, tools and ammunition complete, I'll go ye." So the deal was made and in an hour Josh was home. He stabled Grizzle, the last of their saddle stock, and entered.

Love and sorrow dwelt in the widow's home, but the return of Josh brought its measure of joy. Mother prepared the regular meal of tea, potatoes, and salt pork; there was a time when they had soared as high as canned goods, but those prosperous days were gone. Josh was dandling baby sister on his lap as he told of his trip, and he learned of two things of interest: First, the bank must have its money by February; second, the stable at Gardiner wanted a driver for the Cook City stage. Then the little events moved quickly. His half-formed plan of getting back to the Canyon was now frustrated by the new opening, and, besides this, hope had been dampened by the casual word of one who reported that "that Silver Fox had not been seen since at the Canyon."

Then began long days of dreary driving through the snow, with a noon halt at Yancey's and then three days later the return, in the cold, the biting cold. It was freezing work, but coldest of all was the chill thought at his heart that February 1st would see him homeless.

Small bands of Mountain Sheep he saw at times on the slope of Evarts, and a few Blacktail, and later, when the winter deepened, huge bull Elk were seen along the trail. Sometimes they moved not more than a few paces to let him pass. These were everyday things to him, but in the second week of his winter work he got a sudden thrill. He was coming down the long hill back of Yancey's when what should he see there, sitting on its tail, shiny black with yellow eyes like a huge black cat unusually long and sharp in the nose, but a wonderful Silver Fox! Possibly the same as the one he saw at the Canyon, for that one he knew had disappeared and there were not likely to be two in the Park. Yes, it might be the same, and Josh's bosom surged with mingled feelings. Why did he not carry that little gun? Why did he not realize? Were the thoughts that came--$500! A noble chance! broad daylight only twenty-five yards! and gone!

The Fox was still there when Josh drove on. On the next trip he brought the little rifle. He had sawed off the stock so he could hide it easily in his overcoat if need be. No man knew that he carried arms, but the Foxes seemed to know. The Red ones kept afar and the Black one came no more. Day after day he drove and hoped but the Black Fox has cunning measured to his value. He came not, or if he came, was wisely hidden, and so the month went by, till late in the cold Moon of Snow he heard old Yancey, say "There's a Silver Fox bin a-hanging around the stable this last week. Leastwise Dave says he seen him." There were soldiers sitting around that stove, game guardians of the Park, and still more dangerous, a scout, the soldiers' guide, a mountaineer. Josh turned not an inch, he made no sound in response, but his heart gave a jump. Half an hour later he went out to bed his horses for the night, and peering around the stable he saw a couple of shadowy forms that silently shifted until swallowed by the gloom.

Then the soldiers came to bed their horses, and Josh went back to the stove. His big driving coat hung with the little sawed-off rifle in the long pocket. He waited till the soldiers one by one went up the ladder to the general bunk-room. He rose again, got the lantern, lighted it, carried it out behind the lonely stable. The horses were grinding their hay, the stars were faintly lighting the snow. There was no one about as he hung the lantern under the eaves outside so that it could be seen from the open valley, but not from the house.

A faint Yap-yah, of a Fox was heard on the piney hillside, as he lay down on the hay in the loft, but there were no signs of life on the snow. He had come to wait all night if need be, and waited. The lantern might allure, it might scare, but it was needed in this gloom, and it tinged the snow with faint yellow light below him. An hour went by, then a big-tailed form came near and made a little bark at the lantern. It looked very dark, but it had a paler patch on the throat. This waiting was freezing work; Josh's teeth were chattering in spite of his overcoat. Another gray form came, then a much larger black one shaped itself on the white. It dashed at the first, which fled, and the second one followed but a little, and then sat down on the snow, gazing at that bright light. When you are sure, you are so sure--Josh knew him now, he was facing the Silver Fox. But the light was dim. Josh's hand trembled as he bared it to lay the back on his lips and suck so as to make a mousey squeak. The effect on the Fox was instant. He glided forward intent as a hunting cat. Again he stood in, oh! such a wonderful pose, still as a statue, frozen like a hiding partridge, unbudging as a lone kid Antelope in May. And Josh raised--yes, he had come for that--he raised that fatal gun. The lantern blazed in the Fox's face at twenty yards; the light was flung back doubled by its shining eyes; it looked perfectly clear. Josh lined the gun, but, strange to tell, the sights so plain were lost at once, and the gun was shaking like a sorghum stalk while the Gopher gnaws its root.

He laid the weapon down with a groan, cursed his own poor trembling hand, and in an instant the wonder Fox was gone.

Poor Josh! He wasn't bad-tongued, but now he used all the evil words he had ever heard, and he was Western bred. Then he reacted on himself. "The Fox might come back!" Suddenly he remembered something. He got out a common sulphur match. He wet it on his lips and rubbed it on the muzzle sight: Then on each side of the notch on the breech sight. He lined it for a tree. Yes! surely! What had been a blur of blackness had now a visible form.

A faint bark on a far hillside might mean a coming or a going Fox. Josh waited five minutes, then again he squeaked on his bare hand. The effect was a surprise when from the shelter of the stable wall ten feet below there leaped the great dark Fox. At fifteen feet it paused. Those yellow orbs were fiery in the light and the rifle sights with the specks of fire were lined. There was a sharp report and the black-robed fur was still and limp in the snow.

Who can tell the crack of a small rifle among the louder cracks of green logs splitting with the fierce frost of a Yellowstone winter's night? Why should travel-worn, storm-worn travellers wake at each slight, usual sound? Who knows? Who cares?

* * * * *

And afar in Livingston what did the fur dealer care? It was a great prize--or the banker? he got his five hundred, and mother found it easy to accept the Indians' creed: "Who owns wild beasts? The man who kills them."

"I did not know how it would come," she said; "I only knew it would come, for I prayed and believed."

We know that it came when it meant the most. The house was saved. It was the turn in their fortune's tide, and the crucial moment of the change was when those three bright sulphur spots were lined with the living lamps in the head of the Silver Fox. Yes! Josh was a poacher. Just once.

THE VILLAIN IN VELVET--THE MARTEN

This beautiful animal, the Sable of America, with its rich brown fur and its golden throat, comes naturally after the Silver Fox, for such is the relative value of their respective coats.

The Fox is a small wild dog; the Marten is a large tree Weasel. It is a creature of amazing agility, so much so that it commonly runs down the Red-squirrel among the tree tops.

Its food consists mainly of mice and Squirrels, but it kills Rabbits and Grouse when it can find them, and sometimes even feasts on game of a far more noble size.

Tom Newcomb, my old guide, has given me an interesting note on the Marten, made while he was acting as hunting guide in the Shoshoni Mountains.

In October, 1911, he was out with Baron D' Epsen and his party, hunting on Miller Creek east of Yellowstone Park. They shot at a Deer. It ran off as though unharmed, but turned to run down hill, and soon the snow showed that it was spurting blood on both sides. They followed for three or four hundred yards, and then the Deer track was joined by the tracks of five Marten. In a few minutes they found the Deer down and the five Marten, a family probably, darting about in the near trees, making their peculiar soft purr as though in anticipation of the feast, which was delayed only by the coming of the hunters. These attempts to share with the killers of big game are often seen.

THE INDUSTRIOUS BEAVER

In some respects the Beaver is the most notable animal in the West. It was the search for Beaver skins that led adventurers to explore the Rocky Mountains, and to open up the whole northwest of the United States and Canada. It is the Beaver to-day that is the chief incentive to poachers in the Park, but above all the Beaver is the animal that most manifests its intelligence by its works, forestalls man in much of his best construction, and amazes us by the well-considered labour of its hands.

There was a time when the Beaver's works and wisdom were so new and astounding that super-human intelligence was ascribed to this fur-clad engineer. Then the scoffers came and reduced him to the low level of his near kin, and explained the accounts of his works as mere fairy tales. Now we have got back to the middle of the road. We find him a creature of intelligence far above that of his near kinsmen, and endowed with some extraordinary instincts that guide him in making dams, houses, etc., that are unparalleled in the animal world. Here are the principal deliberate constructions of the Beaver: First the lodge. The Beaver was the original inventor of reinforced concrete. He has used it for a million years, in the form of mud mixed with sticks and stones, for building his lodge and dam. The lodge is the home of the family; that is, it shelters usually one old male, one old female and sundry offspring. It is commonly fifteen to twenty feet across outside, and three to five feet high. Within is a chamber about two feet high and six feet across, well above water and provided with a ventilator through the roof, also two entering passages under water, one winding for ordinary traffic, and one straight for carrying in wood, whose bark is a staple food. This house is kept perfectly tidy, and when the branch is stripped of all eatable parts, it is taken out and worked into the dam, which is a crooked bank of mud and sticks across the running stream. It holds the water so as to moat the Beaver Castle.

But the canal is one of this animal's most interesting undertakings. It is strictly a freight canal for bringing in food-logs, and is dug out across level ground toward the standing timber.

Canals are commonly three or four hundred feet long, about three feet wide and two feet deep. There was a small but good example at Yancey's in 1897; it was only seventy feet long. The longest I ever saw was in the Adirondacks, N. Y.; it was six hundred and fifty-four feet in length following the curves, two or three feet wide and about two feet deep.

Three other Beaver structures should be noticed. One, the dock or plunge hole, which is a deep place by a sharply raised bank, both made with careful manual labour. Next, the sunning place, generally an ant-hill on which the Beaver lies to enjoy a sun-bath, while the ants pick the creepers out of his fur. Third, the mud-pie. This is a little patty of mud mixed with a squeeze of the castor or body-scent glands. It answers the purpose of a register, letting all who call know that so and so has recently been here.

The chief food of the Beaver, at least its favourite food, is aspen, also called quaking asp or poplar; where there are no poplars there are no Beavers.

THE DAM

Usually the Beavers start a dam on some stream, right opposite a good grove of poplars. When these are all cut down and the bark used for food, the Beaver makes a second dam on the same stream, always with a view to having deep water for safety, close by poplars for food. In this way I found the Beavers at Yancey's in 1897 had constructed thirteen dams in succession. But when I examined the ground again in 1912, the dams were broken, the ponds all dry. Why? The answer is very simple. The Beavers had used up all the food. Instead of the little aspen groves there were now nothing but stumps, and the Beavers had moved elsewhere.

Similarly in 1897 the largest Beaver pond in the Park was at Obsidian Cliff. I should say the dam there was over four hundred yards long. But now it is broken and the pond is drained. And the reason as before--the Beavers used all the food and moved on. Of course the dam is soon broken when the hardworking ones are not there in their eternal vigilance to keep it tight.

There are many good Beaver ponds near Yancey's now and probably made by the same colonies of Beavers as those I studied there.

Last September I found a fine lots of dams and dammers on the southeast side of Yellowstone Lake where you may go on a camera hunt with certainty of getting Beaver pictures. Yes, in broad daylight.

Let me correct here some popular errors about the Beaver:

It does not use its tail as a trowel.

It does not use big logs in building a dam.

It does not and cannot drive stakes.

It cannot throw a tree in any given way.

It finishes the lodge outside with sticks, not mud.

THE OTTER AND HIS SLIDE

Every one of us that ever was a small boy and rejoiced in belly-bumping down some icy hill, on a sled of glorious red, should have a brotherly sympathy for the Otter.

While in a large sense this beautiful animal belongs to the Weasel family, it has so far progressed that it is one of the merriest, best-natured, unsanguinary creatures that ever caught their prey alive. This may be largely owing to the fact that it has taken entirely to a fish diet; for without any certain knowledge of the reason, we observe that fisherfolk are gentler than hunterfolk, and the Otter among his Weasel kin affords a good illustration of this.

We find the animals going through much the same stages as we do. First, the struggle for food, then for mates, and later, when they have no cause to worry about either, they seek for entertainment. Quite a number of our animals have invented amusements. Usually these are mere games of tag, catch, or tussle, but some have gone farther and have a regular institution, with a set place to meet, and apparatus provided. This is the highest form of all, and one of the best illustrations of it is found in the jovial Otter. Coasting is an established game with this animal; and probably every individual of the species frequents some Otter slide. This is any convenient steep hill or bank, sloping down into deep water, prepared by much use, and worn into a smooth shoot that becomes especially serviceable when snow or ice are there to act as lightning lubricants. And here the Otters will meet, old and young, male and female, without any thought but the joy of fun together, and shoot down one after the other, swiftly, and swifter still, as the hill grows smooth with use, and plump into the water and out again; and chase each other with little animal gasps of glee, each striving to make the shoot more often and more quickly than the others. And all of this charming scene, this group and their merry game, is unquestionably for the simple social joy of being together in an exercise which gives to them the delicious, exhilarating sensation of speeding through space without either violence or effort. In fact, for the very same reason that you and I went coasting when we were boys.

Do not fail to get one of the guides to show you the Otter slides as you travel about the lake. Some of them are good and some are poor. The very best are seen after the snow has come, but still you can see them with your own eyes, and if you are very lucky and very patient you may be rewarded by the sight of these merry creatures indulging in a game which closely parallels so many of our own.

* * * * *

IV

Horns and Hoofs and Legs of Speed

* * * * *

IV

Horns and Hoofs and Legs of Speed

THE BOUNDING BLACKTAIL

When Lewis and Clark reached the Big Sioux River in Dakota, on their famous journey up the Missouri, one hundred and ten years ago, they met, on the very edge and beginning of its range, the Mule Deer, and added the new species to their collection.

It is the characteristic Deer of the rough country from Mexico to British Columbia, and from California to Manitoba; and is one of the kinds most easily observed in the Yellowstone Sanctuary.

Driving from Gardiner, passing under the Great Tower of Eagle Rock on which an Osprey has nested year after year as far back as the records go, and wheeling into the open space in front of the Mammoth Hot Springs Hotel, one is almost sure to come on a family of Deer wandering across the lawn, or posing among the shrubbery, with all the artless grace of the truly wild creature. These are the representatives of several hundred that collect in fall on and about this lawn, but are now scattered for the summer season over the adjoining hills, to come again, no doubt in increased numbers, when the first deep snow shall warn them to seek their winter range.

Like the other animals, these are natives of the region and truly wild, but so educated by long letting alone that it is easy to approach within a few yards.

The camera hunter should not fail to use this opportunity, not only because they are wild and beautiful things, but because he can have the films developed at the hotel over night, and so find out how his camera is behaving in this new light and surroundings.

This is the common Blacktailed Deer of the hill country, called Mule Deer on account of its huge ears and the shape of its tail. In Canada I knew it by the name of "Jumping Deer," from its gait, and in the Rockies it is familiar as the "Bounding Blacktail"--"Bounding" because of the wonderful way in which it strikes the ground with its legs held stiffly, then rises in the air with little apparent effort, and lands some ten or fifteen feet away. As the hunters say,

"The Blacktail hits only the high places in the landscape." On the level it does not run so well as the Antelope or the Whitetailed Deer, and I often wondered why it had adopted this laborious mode of speeding, which seemed so inferior to the normal pace of its kin. But at length I was eyewitness of an episode that explained the puzzle.

THE MOTHER BLACKTAIL'S RACE FOR LIFE

In the fall of 1897 I was out for a Wolf hunt with the Eaton boys in the Badlands near Medora, N. D. We had a fine mixed pack of dogs, trailers, runners, and fighters. The runners were thoroughbred greyhounds, that could catch any four-foot on the plains except perhaps a buck Antelope; that I saw them signally fail in. But a Wolf, or even the swift Coyote, had no chance of getting away from them provided they could keep him in view. We started one of these singers of the plains, and at first he set off trusting to his legs, but the greyhounds were after him, and when he saw his long start shrinking so fearfully fast he knew that his legs could not save him, that now was the time for wits to enter the game. And this entry he made quickly and successfully by dropping out of sight down a brushy canyon, so the greyhounds saw him no more.

Then they were baffled by Prairie-dogs which dodged down out of reach and hawks which rose up out of reach, and still we rode, till, rounding a little knoll near a drinking place, we came suddenly on a mother Blacktail and her two fawns. All three swung their big ears and eyes into full bearing on us, and we reined our horses and tried to check our dogs, hoping they had not seen the quarry that we did not wish to harm. But Bran the leader gave a yelp, then leaping high over the sage, directed all the rest, and in a flash it was a life and death race.

Again and frantically the elder Eaton yelled "Come back!" and his brother tried to cut across and intercept the hounds. But a creature that runs away is an irresistible bait to a greyhound, and the chase across the sage-covered flat was on, with every nerve and tendon strained.

Away went the Blacktail, bounding, bounding at that famous beautiful, birdlike, soaring pace, mother and young tapping the ground and sailing to land, and tap and sail again. And away went the greyhounds, low coursing, outstretched, bounding like bolts from a crossbow, curving but little and dropping only to be shot again. They were straining hard; the Blacktail seemed to be going more easily, far more beautifully. But alas! they were losing time. The greyhounds were closing; in vain we yelled at them. We spurred our horses, hoping to cut them off, hoping to stop the ugly, lawless tragedy. But the greyhounds were frantic now. The distance between Bran and the hindmost fawn was not forty feet. Then Eaton drew his revolver and fired shots over the greyhounds' heads, hoping to scare them into submission, but they seemed to draw fresh stimulus from each report, and yelped and bounded faster. A little more and the end would be. Then we saw a touching sight. The hindmost fawn let out a feeble bleat of distress, and the mother, heeding, dropped back between. It looked like choosing death, for now she had not twenty feet of lead. I wanted Eaton to use his gun on the foremost hound, when something unexpected happened. The flat was crossed, the Blacktail reached a great high butte, and tapping with their toes they soared some fifteen feet and tapped again; and tapped and tapped and soared, and so they went like hawks that are bounding in the air, and the greyhounds, peerless on the plain, were helpless on the butte. Yes! rush as they might and did, and bounded and clomb, but theirs was not the way of the hills. In twenty heartbeats they were left behind. The Blacktail mother with her twins kept on and soared and lightly soared till lost to view, and all were safely hidden in their native hills.

THE BLACKTAIL'S SAFETY IS IN THE HILLS

That day I learned the reason for the bounding flight, so beautiful, but not the best or swiftest on the plain, yet the one that gives them dominion and safety on the hills, that makes of them a hill folk that the dangers of the plain can never reach.

So now, O traveller in the Park, if you approach too near the Blacktail feeding near the great hotel, and so alarm them--for they are truly wild--they make not for the open run as do the Antelope and the Hares, not for the thickest bottomland as do the Whitetail and the Lynxes, but for the steeper hillsides. They know right well where their safety lies, and on that near and bushy bank, laying aside all alarm, they group and pose in artless grace that tempts one to a lavish use of films and gives the chance for that crowning triumph of the art, a wild animal group, none of which is looking at the camera.

One more characteristic incident: In 1897 I was riding, with my wife, from Yancey's over to Baronett's Bridge, when we came on a young buck Blacktail. Now, said I, "I am going to show you the most wonderful and beautiful thing to be seen in the way of wild life speeding. You shall now see the famous bounding of the Blacktail." Then I spurred out after the young buck, knowing that all he needed was a little alarm to make him perform. Did he take alarm and run? Not at all. He was in the Yellowstone Sanctuary. He knew nothing of guns or dogs; he had lived all his life in safety. He would trot a few steps out of my way, then turn and gaze at me, but run, bound, and make for the high land, not a bit of it. And to this day my fair companion has not seen the Blacktail bounding up the hills.

THE ELK OR WAPITI--THE NOBLEST OF ALL DEER

The Rocky Mountain Elk, or Wapiti, is the finest of all true Deer. The cows weigh 400 to 500 pounds, the bulls 600 or 800, but occasionally 1000. At several of the hotels a small herd is kept in a corral for the pleasure and photography of visitors.

The latest official census puts the summer population of Elk in the Yellowstone Park at 35,000, but the species is migratory, at least to the extent of seeking a winter feeding ground with as little snow as possible, so that most of them move out as snow time sets in. Small herds linger in the rich and sheltered valleys along the Yellowstone, Snake and nearby rivers, but the total of those wintering in the Park is probably less than 5,000.

STALKING A BAND OF ELK

In the summer months the best places in which to look for these Deer are all the higher forests, especially along the timber-line. I had an interesting stalk after a large band of them among the woods of Tower Falls in the June of 1897. I had found the trail of a considerable herd and followed it up the mountain till the "sign" was fresh. Then I tied up my horse and went forward on foot. For these animals are sufficiently acquainted with man as a mischief-maker to be vigilant in avoiding him, even in the Park. I was cautiously crawling from tree to tree, when out across an open space I descried a cow

Elk and her calf lying down. A little more crawling and I sighted a herd all lying down and chewing the cud. About twenty yards away was a stump whose shelter offered chances to use the camera, but my present position promised nothing, so I set out carefully to cross the intervening space in plain view of scores of Elk; and all would have been well but for a pair of mischievous little Chipmunks. They started a most noisy demonstration against my approach, running back and forth across my path, twittering and flashing their tails about. In vain I prayed for a paralytic stroke to fall on my small tormentors. Their aggravating plan, if plan it was, they succeeded in fully carrying out. The Elk turned all their megaphone ears, their funnel noses and their blazing telescopic eyes my way. I lay like a log and waited; so did they. Then the mountain breeze veered suddenly and bore the taint of man to those watchful mothers. They sprang to their feet, some fifty head at least, half of them with calves by their sides, and away they dashed with a roaring sound, and a rattling and crashing of branches that is wonderfully impressive to hear, and nothing at all to tell about.

I had made one or two rough sketches as I lay on the ground, but the photographs were failures.

This band contained only cows engaged in growing their calves. According to Elk etiquette, the bulls are off by themselves at a much higher elevation, engaged in the equally engrossing occupation of growing their antlers. Most persons are surprised greatly when first they learn that the huge antlers of the Elk, as with most deer, are grown and shed each year. It takes only five months to grow them. They are perfect in late September for the fighting season, and are shed in March. The bull Elk now shapes his conduct to his weaponless condition. He becomes as meek as he was warlike. And so far from battling with all of their own sex that come near, these big "moollys" gather in friendly stag-parties on a basis of equal loss, and haunt the upper woods whose pasture is rich enough to furnish the high power nutriment needed to offset the exhausting drain of growing such mighty horns in such minimum time.

They are more free from flies too in these high places, which is important, for even the antlers are sensitive while growing. They are even more sensitive than the rest of the body, besides being less protected and more temptingly filled with blood. A mosquito would surely think he had struck it rich if he landed on the hot, palpitating end of a Wapiti's thin-skinned, blood-gorged antlers. It is quite probable that some of the queer bumps we see on the finished weapons are due to mosquito or fly stings suffered in the early period of formation.

THE BUGLING ELK

During the summer the bulls attend strictly to their self-development, but late August sees them ready to seek once more the mixed society of their kind. Their horns are fully grown, but are not quite hardened and are still covered with velvet. By the end of September these weapons are hard and cleaned and ready for use, just as a thrilling change sets in in the body and mind of the bull. He is full of strength and vigour, his coat is sleek, his neck is swollen, his muscles are tense, his horns are clean, sharp, and strong, and at their heaviest. A burning ambition to distinguish himself in war, and win favours from the shy ladies of his kind, grows in him to a perfect insanity; goaded by desire, boiling with animal force, and raging with war-lust, he mounts some ridge in the valley and pours forth his very soul in a wild far-reaching battle-cry. Beginning low and rising in pitch to a veritable scream of piercing intensity, it falls to a rumbled growl, which broken into shorter growls dies slowly away. This is the famed bugling of the Elk, and however grotesque it may seem when heard in a zoo, is admitted by all who know it in its homeland to be the most inspiring music in nature--because of what it means. Here is this magnificent creature, big as a horse, strong as a bull, and fierce as a lion, standing in all the pride and glory of his primest prime, announcing to all the world: "I am out for a fight! Do any of you want a F-I-G-H-T----!-!-!?" Nor does he usually have long to wait. From some far mountainside the answer comes:

"Yes, yes, yes! Yes, I Do, Do, Do, Do!"

A few more bugle blasts and the two great giants meet; and when they do, all the world knows it for a mile around, without it being seen. The crashing of the antlers as they close, the roars of hate, the squeals of combat, the cracking of breaking branches as they charge and charge, and push and strive, and--sometimes the thud of a heavy body going down.

Many a time have I heard them in the distant woods, but mostly at night.

Often have I gone forth warily hoping to see something of the fight, for we all love to see a fight when not personally in danger; but luck has been against me. I have been on the battlefield next morning to see where the combatants had torn up an acre of ground, and trampled unnumbered saplings, or tossed huge boulders about like pebbles, but the fight I missed.

One day as I came into camp in the Shoshonees, east of the Park, an old hunter said: "Say, you! you want to see a real old-time Elk fight? You go up on that ridge back of the corral and you'll sure see a hull bunch of 'em at it; not one pair of bulls, but six of 'em."

I hurried away, but again I was too late; I saw nothing but the trampled ground, the broken saplings, and the traces of the turmoil; the battling giants were gone.

Back I went and from the hunter's description made the sketch which I give below. The old man said: "Well, you sure got it this time. That's exactly like it was. One pair was jest foolin', one was fencing and was still perlite; but that third pair was a playin' the game for keeps. An' for givin' the facts, that's away ahead of any photograph I ever seen."

Once I did come on the fatal battle-ground, but it was some time after the decision; and there I found the body of the one who did not win. The antlers are a fair index of the size and vigour of the stag, and if the fallen one was so big and strong, what like was he who downed him, pierced him through and left him on the plain.

SNAPPING A CHARGING BULL

At one time in a Californian Park I heard the war-bugle of an Elk. He bawled aloud in brazen, ringing tones: "Anybody want a F-I-G-H-T t-t-t-t!!"

I extemporized a horn and answered him according to his mood. "Yes, I do; bring it ALONG!" and he brought it at a trot, squealing and roaring as he came. When he got within forty yards he left the cover and approached me, a perfect incarnation of brute ferocity and hate.

His ears were laid back, his muzzle raised, his nose curled up, his lower teeth exposed, his mane was bristling and in his eyes there blazed a marvellous fire of changing opalescent green. On he marched, gritting his teeth and uttering a most unpleasantly wicked squeal.

Then suddenly down went his head, and he came crash at me, with all the power of half a ton of hate. However, I was not so much exposed as may have been inferred. I was safely up a tree. And there I sat watching that crazy bull as he prodded the trunk with his horns, and snorted, and raved around, telling me just what he thought of me, inviting him to a fight and then getting up a tree. Finally he went off roaring and gritting his teeth, but turning back to cast on me from time to time the deadly, opaque green light of his mad, malignant eyes.

A friend of mine, John Fossum, once a soldier attached to Fort Yellowstone, had a similar adventure on a more heroic scale. While out on a camera hunt in early winter he descried afar a large bull Elk lying asleep in an open valley. At once Fossum made a plan. He saw that he could crawl up to the bull, snap him where he lay, then later secure a second picture as the creature ran for the timber. The first part of the programme was carried out admirably. Fossum got within fifty feet and still the Elk lay sleeping. Then the camera was opened out. But alas! that little pesky "click," that does so much mischief, awoke the bull, who at once sprang to his feet and ran--not for the woods-- but for the man. Fossum with the most amazing nerve stood there quietly focussing his camera, till the bull was within ten feet, then pressed the button, threw the camera into the soft snow and ran for his life with the bull at his coat-tails. It would have been a short run but for the fact that they reached a deep snowdrift that would carry the man, and would not carry the Elk. Here Fossum escaped, while the bull snorted around, telling just what he meant to do to the man when he caught him; but he was not to be caught, and at last the bull went off grumbling and squealing.

The hunter came back, recovered his camera, and when the plate was developed it bore the picture No. xiv, b.

It shows plainly the fighting light in the bull's eye, the back laid ears, the twisting of the nose, and the rate at which he is coming is evidenced in the stamping feet and the wind-blown whiskers, and yet in spite of the peril of the moment, and the fact that this was a hand camera, there is no sign of shake on landscape or on Elk, and the picture is actually over-exposed.

THE HOODOO COW

One of the best summer ranges for Elk is near the southeast corner of the Yellowstone Lake, and here it was my luck to have the curious experience that I call the "Story of a Hoodoo Elk."

In the September of 1912, when out with Tom Newcomb of Gardiner, I had this curious adventure, that I shall not try to explain. We had crossed the Yellowstone Lake in a motor boat and were camped on the extreme southeast Finger, at a point twenty-five miles as the crow flies, and over fifty as the trail goes, from any human dwelling. We were in the least travelled and most primitive part of the Park. The animals here are absolutely in the wild condition and there was no one in the region but ourselves.

On Friday, September 6th, we sighted some Elk on the lake shore at sunrise, but could not get nearer than two hundred yards, at which distance I took a poor snap. The Elk wheeled and ran out of sight. I set off on foot with the guide about 8:30. We startled one or two Elk, but they were very wild, and I got no chance to photograph.

About 10:30, when several miles farther in the wilderness, we sighted a cow Elk standing in a meadow with a Coyote sneaking around about one hundred yards away. "That's my Elk," I said, and we swung under cover. By keeping in a little pine woods, I got within one hundred yards, taking picture No. 1, Plate XV. As she did not move, I said to Tom: "You stay here while I creep out to that sage brush and I'll get a picture of her at fifty yards." By crawling on my hands I was able to do this and got picture No. 2. Now I noticed a bank of tall grass some thirty yards from the cow, and as she was still quiet, I crawled to that and got picture No. 3. She did not move and I was near enough to see that she was dozing in a sun-bath. So I stood up and beckoned to Tom to come out of the woods at once. He came on nearly speechless with amazement. "What is the meaning of this?" he whispered.

I replied calmly: "I told you I was a medicine man, perhaps you'll believe me now. Don't you see I've made Elk medicine and got her hypnotized? Now I am going to get up to about twenty yards and take her picture. While I do so, you use the second camera and take me in the act." So Tom took No. 4 while I was taking No. 5, and later No. 6.

"Now," I said, "let's go and talk to her." We walked up to within ten yards. The Elk did not move, so I said: "Well, Bossie, you have callers. Won't you please look this way?" She did so and I secured shot No. 7, Plate XVI.

"Thank you," I said. "Now be good enough to lie down." She did, and I took No. 9.

I went up and stroked her, so did Tom; then giving her a nudge of my foot I said: "Now stand up again and look away."

She rose up, giving me Nos. 8, 10 and 11.

"Thank you, Bossie! now you can go!" And as she went off I fired my last film, getting No. 12.

By this time Tom had used up all his allowable words, and was falling back on the contraband kind to express his surging emotions.

"What the ---- is the ---- meaning ---- of this ----?" and so on.

I replied calmly: "Maybe you'll believe I have Elk medicine. Now show me a Moose and I'll give you some new shocks."

Our trip homeward occupied a couple of hours, during which I heard little from Tom but a snort or two of puzzlement.

As we neared camp he turned on me suddenly and said: "Now, Mr. Seton, what is the meaning of this? That wasn't a sick Elk; she was fat and hearty. She wasn't poisoned or doped, 'cause there's no possibility of that. It wasn't a tame Elk, 'cause there ain't any, and, anyhow, we're seventy miles from a house. Now what is the meaning of it?"

I replied solemnly: "Tom! I don't know any more than you do. I was as much surprised as you were at everything but one, and that was when she lay down. I didn't tell her to lie down till I saw she was going to do it, or to get up either, or look the other way, and if you can explain the incident, you've got the field to yourself."

THE MOOSE, THE BIGGEST OF ALL DEER

The Moose is one of the fine animals that have responded magnificently to protection in Canada, Maine, Minnesota, and the Yellowstone Park. Formerly they were very scarce in Wyoming and confined to the southwest corner of the Reserve. But all they needed was a little help; and, receiving it, they have flourished and multiplied. Their numbers have grown by natural increase from about fifty in 1897 to some five hundred and fifty to-day; and they have spread into all the southern half of the Park wherever they find surroundings to their taste; that is, thick level woods with a mixture of timber, as the Moose is a brush-eater, and does not flourish on a straight diet of evergreen.

The first Deer, almost the only one I ever killed, was a Moose and that was far back in the days of my youth. On the Yellowstone, I am sorry to say, I never saw one, although I found tracks and signs in abundance last September near the Lake.

MY PARTNER'S MOOSE-HUNT

Though I have never since fired at a Moose, I was implicated in the killing of one a few years later.

It was in the fall of the year, in the Hunting Moon, I was in the Kippewa Country with my partner and some chosen friends on a camping trip. Our companions were keen to get a Moose; and daily all hands but myself were out with the expert Moose callers. But each night the company reassembled around the campfire only to exchange their stories of failure.

Moose there were in plenty, and good guides, Indian, halfbreed and white, but luck was against them all. Without being a very expert caller I have done enough of it to know the game and to pass for a "caller." So one night I said in a spirit of half jest: "I'll have to go out and show you men how to call a Moose." I cut a good piece of birch-bark and fashioned carefully a horn. Disdaining all civilized materials as "bad medicine," I stitched the edge with a spruce root or wattap, and soldered it neatly with pine gum flowed and smoothed with a blazing brand. And then I added the finishing touch, a touch which made the Indian and the halfbreed shake their heads ominously; I drew two "hoodoo Moose"--that is, men with Moose heads dancing around the horn.

THE SIREN CALL

"You put that on before you catch one Moose, Moose never come," they said.

Still I put them on, and near sundown set off in a canoe, with one guide as paddler, and my partner in charge of the only gun. In half an hour we reached a lonely lake surrounded by swamps, and woods of mixed timber. The sunset red was purpling all the horizon belt of pines, and the peace of the still hour was on lake and swamp. With some little sense of profanity I raised the hoodoo horn to my mouth, gave one or two high-pitched, impatient grunts, then poured forth the softly rising, long-drawn love-call of a cow Moose, all alone, and "Oh, so lonesome."

The guide nodded in approval, "That's all right," then I took out my watch and waited for fifteen minutes. For, strange to tell, it seems to repel the bull Moose and alarm him if the cow seems over-eager. There is a certain etiquette to be observed; it is easy to spoil all by trying to go too fast. And it does not do to guess at the time; when one is waiting so hard, the minute is like twenty.

So when fifteen minutes really had gone, I raised the magic horn again, emitted a few hankering whines, then broke into a louder, farther reaching call that thrilled up echoes from across the lake and seemed to fill the woods for miles around with its mellifluous pleading.

Again I waited and gave a third call just as the sun was gone. Then we strained our eyes and watched at every line of woods, and still were watching when the sound of a falling tree was heard far off on a hillside.

Then there was a sort of after-clap as though the tree had lodged the first time, and hanging half a minute, had completed its fall with breaking of many branches, and a muffled crash. We gazed hard that way, and the guide, a very young one, whispered, "Bear!"

There was silence, then a stick broke nearer, and a deep, slow snort was heard; it might have been the "woof" of a Bear, but I was in doubt. Then without any more noises, a white array of shining antler tips appeared above the near willows, and swiftly, silently, there glided into view a huge bull Moose.

"How solid and beefy he looks!" was my first thought. He "woofed" again, and the guide, with an eye always to the head, whispered to my partner: "Take him! he's a stunner."

Striding on he came, with wonderful directness, seeing I had not called for twenty minutes, and that when he was a mile or more away.

As he approached within forty yards, the guide whispered, "Now is your chance. You'll never get a better one." My partner whispered, "Steady the canoe." I drove my paddle point into the sandy bottom, the guide did the same at the other end, and she arose standing in the canoe and aimed. Then came the wicked "crack" of the rifle, the "pat" of the bullet, the snort and whirl of the great, gray, looming brute, and a second shot as he reached the willows, only to go down with a crash, and sob his life out on the ground behind the leafy screen.

It all seemed so natural, so exactly according to the correct rules of sporting books and tales, and yet so unlovely.

There were tears in the eyes of the fair killer, and heart wrenches were hers, as the great sobs grew less and ceased; and a different sob was heard at my elbow, as we stood beside the biggest Moose that had been killed there in years. It was triumph I suppose; it is a proud thing to act a lie so cleverly; the Florentine assassins often decoyed and trapped a brave man, by crying like a woman. But I have never called a Moose since, and that rifle has hung unused in its rack from that to the present day.

THE BIGGEST OF OUR GAME--THE BUFFALO

"Yes, that's a buffalo-bird," said the old Indian, pointing to some black birds, with gray mates, that flitted or ran across the plain. "Pretty bad luck when the Buffalo gone. Them little birds make their nest in a Buffalo's wool, right on his head, and when the Buffalo all gone, seem like the buffalo-bird die too; 'cause what's the use, no got any nest."

This is a fragment that reached me long ago in Montana. It seemed like a lusty myth, whose succulent and searching roots were in a bottomless bog, with little chance of sound foundation. But the tale bore the searchlight better than I thought. For it seems that the buffalo-bird followed the Buffalo everywhere, and was fond of nesting, not in the shaggy mane between the horns of the ruling monarch, but on any huge head it might find after the bull had fallen, and the skull, with mane attached, lay discarded on the plain. While always, even when nesting on the ground, the wool of the Buffalo was probably used as lining of the black-bird's nest. I know of one case where an attendant bird that was too crippled to fly when autumn came, wintered in the mane of a large Buffalo bull. It gathered seed by day, when the bull pawed up the snow, and roosted at night between the mighty horns, snuggling in the wool, with its toes held warm against the monster's blood-hot neck.

In most of the Northwest the birds have found a poor substitute for the Buffalo in the range-cattle, but oh! how they must miss the wool.

THE SHRUNKEN RANGE

It is not generally known that the American Buffalo ranged as far east as Syracuse, Washington City, and Carolina, that they populated the forests in small numbers, as well as the plains in great herds. I estimate them at over 50,000,000 in A.D. 1500. In 1895 they were down to 800; probably this was the low-ebb year. Since then they have increased under judicious protection, and now reach about 3,000.

In the June of 1897, as I stood on a hill near Baronett's Bridge, overlooking the Yellowstone just beyond Yancey's, with an old timer, Dave Roberts, he said: "Twenty years ago, when I first saw this valley, it was black-speckled with Buffalo, and every valley in the Park was the same." Now the only sign of the species was a couple of old skulls crumbling in the grass.

In 1900 the remnant in the Park had fallen to thirty, and their extinction seemed certain. But the matter was taken up energetically by the officers in charge. Protection, formerly a legal fiction, was made an accomplished fact. The Buffalo have increased ever since, and to-day number 200, with the possibility of some stragglers.

We need not dwell on the story of the extinction of the great herds. That is familiar to all,[B] but it is well to remind the reader that it was inevitable. The land was, or would be, needed for human settlement, with which the Buffalo herds were incompatible; only we brought it on forty or fifty years before it was necessary. "Could we not save the Buffalo as range-cattle?" is the question that most ask. The answer is: It has been tried a hundred times and all attempts have been eventually frustrated by the creature's temper. Buffalo, male or female, are always more or less dangerous; they cannot be tamed or trusted. They are always subject to stampede, and once started, nothing, not even sure destruction, stops them; so in spite of their suitability to the climate, their hardihood, their delicious meat, and their valuable robes, the attempts at domesticating the Buffalo have not yet been made a success.

A small herd of a dozen or so is kept in a fenced range near the Mammoth Hot Springs, where the traveller should not fail to try for pictures, and with them he will see the cowbirds, that in some regions replace the true buffalo-birds. Perched on their backs or heads or running around them on the ground are these cattle birds as of yore, like boats around a man-o'-war, or sea-gulls around a whale; living their lives, snapping up the tormenting flies, and getting in return complete protection from every creature big enough to seem a menace in the eyes of the old time King of the Plains.

THE DOOMED ANTELOPE AND HIS HELIOGRAPH

The Antelope, or Pronghorn, is one of the most peculiar animals in the world. It is the only known ruminant that has hollow horns on a bony core as with cattle, and also has them branched and shed each year as in the Deer.

It is a creature of strangely mixed characteristics, for it has the feet of a Giraffe, the glands of a goat, the coat of a Deer, the horns of an ox and Deer combined, the eyes of a Gazelle, the build of an Antelope, and--the speed of the wind. It is the swiftest four-footed creature native to the plains, and so far as known there is nothing but a blooded race horse that can outrun it on a mile.

But the peculiarity that is most likely to catch the eye of the traveller is the white disc on its rear.

The first day I was in the Yellowstone I was riding along the upland beyond Blacktail Creek with T. E. Hofer. Miles away to the southeast we saw some white specks showing, flashing and disappearing. Then as far to the northeasterly we saw others. Hofer now remarked, "Two bunches of Antelope." Then later there were flashes between and we knew that these two bands had come together. How?

When you have a chance in a zoo or elsewhere to watch Antelope at short range you will see the cause of these flashes. By means of a circular muscle on each buttock they can erect the white hair of the rump patch into a large, flat, snow-white disc which shines in the sun, and shows afar as a bright white spot.

This action is momentary or very brief; the spread disc goes down again in a few seconds. The flash is usually a signal of danger, although it answers equally well for a recognition mark.

In 1897 the Antelope in the Park were estimated at 1,500. Now they have dwindled to about one third of that, and, in spite of good protection, continue to go down. They do not flourish when confined even in a large area, and we have reason to fear that one of the obscure inexorable laws of nature is working now to shelve the Antelope with the creatures that have passed away. A small band is yet to be seen wintering on the prairie near Gardiner.

THE RESCUED BIGHORN

At one time the Bighorn abounded along all the rivers where there was rough land as far east as the western edge of the Dakotas, westerly to the Cascades, and in the mountains from Mexico and Southern California to Alaska.

In one form or another the Mountain Sheep covered this large region, and it is safe to say that in the United States alone their numbers were millions. But the dreadful age of the repeating rifle and lawless skin-hunter came on, till the end of the last century saw the Bighorn in the United States reduced to a few hundreds; they were well along the sunset trail.

But the New York Zoological Society, the Camp Fire Club, and other societies of naturalists and sportsmen, bestirred themselves mightily. They aroused all thinking men to the threatening danger of extinction; good laws were passed and then enforced. The danger having been realized, the calamity was averted, and now the Sheep are on the increase in many parts of the West.

During the epoch of remorseless destruction the few survivors were the wildest of wild things; they would not permit the approach of a man within a mile. But our new way of looking at the Bighorn has taught them a new way of looking at us, as every traveller in Colorado or the protected parts of Wyoming will testify.

In 1897 I spent several months rambling on the upper ranges of the Yellowstone Park, and I saw not a single Sheep, although it was estimated that there were nearly a hundred of the scared fugitives hiding and flying among the rocks.

In 1912 it was believed that in spite of poachers, Cougars, snow slides, and scab contracted from domestic sheep, the Bighorn in the Yellowstone Park had increased to considerably over two hundred, and the traveller can find them with fair certainty if he will devote a few days to the quest around Mt. Evarts, Washburn, or the well-known ranges.

In September, 1912, I left Gardiner with Tom Newcomb's outfit. I was riding at the end of the procession watching in all directions, when far up on the slide rock I caught sight of a Sheep. A brief climb brought me within plain though not near view, to learn that there were half a dozen at least, and I took a few shots with my camera. I think there were many more hidden in the tall sage behind, but I avoided alarming them, so did not find out.

There were neither rams nor lambs with this herd of ewes. The rams keep their own company all summer and live, doubtless, far higher in the mountains.

On Mt. Washburn a week later I had the luck to find a dozen ewes with their lambs; but the sky was dark with leaden clouds and the light so poor that I got no good results.

In winter, as I learn from Colonel Brett, the Sheep are found in small bands between the Mammoth Hot Springs and Gardiner, for there is good feed there, and far less snow than in the upper ranges. I have just heard that this winter four great rams are seen there every day with about forty other Sheep; and they are so tame that one can get pictures within ten feet if desired. Alas! that I have to be so far away with such thrilling opportunities going to waste.

FOOTNOTES:

[Footnote B: See "Life Histories of Northern Animals," by E. T. Seton.]

* * * * *

V

Bats in the Devil's Kitchen

* * * * *

V

Bats in the Devil's Kitchen

It is unfortunate that the average person has a deep prejudice against the Bat. Without looking or thinking for himself, he accepts a lot of absurd tales about the winged one, and passes them on and on, never caring for the injustice he does or the pleasure he loses. I have loved the Bat ever since I came to know him; that is, all my mature life. He is the climax of creation in many things, highly developed in brain, marvellously keen in senses, clad in exquisite fur and equipped, above all, with the crowning glory of flight. He is the prototype and the realization of the Fairy of the Wood we loved so much as children, and so hated to be robbed of by grown-ups, who should have known better.

I would give a good deal to have a Bat colony where I could see it daily, and would go a long way to meet some new kind of Bat.

I never took much interest in caverns, or geysers, or in any of the abominable cavities of the earth that nature so plainly meant to keep hidden from our eyes. I shall not forget the unpleasant sensations I had when first, in 1897, I visited the Yellowstone Wonderland and stood gazing at that abominable Mud Geyser, which is even worse to-day. The entry in my journal of the time runs thus:

"The Mud Geyser is unlike anything that can be seen elsewhere. One hears about the bowels of the earth; this surely is the end of one of them. They talk of the mouth of hell; this is the mouth with a severe fit of vomiting. The filthy muck is spewed from an unseen gullet at one side into a huge upright mouth with sounds of oozing, retching and belching. Then as quickly reswallowed with noises expressive of loathing on its own part, while noxious steam spreads disgusting, unpleasant odours all around. The whole process is quickly repeated, and goes on and on, and has gone on for ages, and will go. And yet one feels that this is merely the steam vent outside of the huge factory where all the actual work is being done. One does not really see the thing at all, but only stands outside the building where it is going on. One never wishes to see it a second time. All are disgusted by it, but all are fascinated."

* * * * *

No, I like them not. I have a natural antipathy to the internal arrangements of Mother Earth. I might almost say a delicacy about gazing on such exposure. Anyhow, we shall all get underground soon enough; and I usually drop off when our party prepares to explore dark, horrible, smelly underground places that have no possible claim (I hold) for the normal being of healthy instincts.

But near the Mammoth Hot Springs is a hellhole that did attract me. It is nothing else than the stuffy, blind alley known as the Devil's Kitchen. There is no cooking going on at present, probably because it is not heated up enough, but there is a peculiarly hot, close feeling suggestive of the Monkey house in an old-time zoo. I went down this, not that I was interested in the Satanic cuisine, but because my ancient antipathy was routed by my later predilection--I was told that Bats "occurred" in the kitchen. Sure enough, I found them, half a dozen, so far as one could tell in the gloom, and thanks to the Park Superintendent, Colonel L. M. Brett, I secured a specimen which, to my great surprise, turned out to be the long-eared Bat, a Southern species never before discovered north of Colorado. It will be interesting to know whether they winter here or go south, as do many of their kin. They would have to go a long way before they would find another bedroom so warm and safe. Even if they go as far as the equator, with its warmth and its pests, they would probably have reason to believe that the happiest nights of their lives were those spent in the Devil's Kitchen.

* * * * *

VI

The Well-meaning Skunk

* * * * *

VI

The Well-meaning Skunk

I have a profound admiration for the Skunk. Indeed, I once maintained that this animal was the proper emblem of America. It is, first of all, peculiar to this continent. It has stars on its head and stripes on its body. It is an ideal citizen; minds its own business, harms no one, and is habitually inoffensive, as long as it is left alone; but it will face any one or any number when aroused. It has a wonderful natural ability to take the offensive; and no man ever yet came to grips with a Skunk without being sadly sorry for it afterward.

Nevertheless, in spite of all this, and the fact that several other countries have prior claims on the Eagle, I could not secure, for my view, sufficient popular support to change the national emblem.

From Atlantic to Pacific and from Mexico far north into the wilds of Canada the Skunk is found, varying with climate in size and colour indeed, but everywhere the same in character and in mode of defense.

It abounds in the broken country that lies between forest and prairie, but seems to avoid the thicker woods as well as the higher peaks.

In Yellowstone Park it is not common, but is found occasionally about Mammoth Hot Springs and Yancey's, at which latter place I had much pleasant acquaintance with its kind.

HIS SMELL-GUN

Every one knows that the animal can make a horrible smell in defending itself, but most persons do not realize what the smell is, or how it is made. First of all, and this should be in capitals, it has nothing at all to do with the kidneys or with the sex organs. It is simply a highly specialized musk secreted by a gland, or rather, a pair of them, located under the tail. It is used for defense when the Skunk is in peril of his life, or thinks he is. But a Skunk may pass his whole life without using it.

He can throw it to a distance of seven to ten feet according to his power or the wind. If it reaches the eyes of his assailant it blinds him temporarily. If it enters his mouth it sets up a frightful nausea. If the vapour gets into his lungs, it chokes as well as nauseates. There are cases on record of men and dogs being permanently blinded by this awful spray. And there is one case of a boy being killed by it.

Most Americans know somewhat of its terrors, but few of them realize the harmlessness of the Skunk when let alone. In remote places I find men who still think that this creature goes about shooting as wildly and wantonly as any drunken cowboy.

THE CRUELTY OF STEEL TRAPS

A few days ago while walking with a friend in the woods we came on a Skunk. My companion shouted to the dog and captured him to save him from a possible disaster, then called to me to keep back and let the Skunk run away. But the fearless one in sable and ermine did not run, and I did not keep back, but I walked up very gently. The Skunk stood his ground and raised his tail high over his back, the sign of fight. I talked to him, still drawing nearer; then, when only ten feet away, was surprised to see that one of his feet was in a trap and terribly mangled.

I stooped down, saying many pleasant things about my friendliness, etc. The Skunk's tail slowly lowered and I came closer up. Still, I did not care to handle the wild and tormented thing on such short acquaintance, so I got a small barrel and quietly placed it over him, then removed the trap and brought him home, where he is now living in peace and comfort.

I mention this to show how gentle and judicious a creature the Skunk is when gently and judiciously approached. It is a sad commentary on our modes of dealing with wild life when I add that as afterward appeared this Skunk had been struggling in the tortures of that trap for three days and three nights.

FRIENDLINESS OF THE SKUNK

These remarks are preliminary to an account of my adventures with a family of Skunks in the Park. During the summer I spent in the little shanty still to be seen, opposite Yancey's, I lost no opportunity of making animal investigations. One of my methods was to sweep the dust on the trail and about the cabin quite smooth at night so that any creature passing should leave me his tracks and I should be sure that they were recent.

One morning on going out I found the fresh tracks of a Skunk. Next night these were seen again, in fact, there were two sets of them. A day or so later the cook at the nearby log hotel announced that a couple of Skunks came every evening to feed at the garbage bucket outside the kitchen door. That night I was watching for them. About dusk one came, walking along sedately with his tail at half mast. The house dog and the house cat both were at the door as the Skunk arrived. They glanced at the newcomer; then the cat discreetly went indoors and the dog rumbled in his chest, but discreetly he walked away, very stiffly, and looked at the distant landscape, with his hair on his back still bristling. The Skunk waddled up to the garbage pail, climbed in, though I was but ten feet away, and began his evening meal.

Another came later. Their tails were spread and at each sharp noise rose a little higher, but no one offered them harm, and they went their way when they were filled.

After this it was a regular thing to go out and see the Skunks feed when evening came.

PHOTOGRAPHING SKUNKS AT SHORT RANGE

I was anxious to get a picture or two, but was prevented by the poor light; in fact, it was but half light, and in those days we had no brilliant flash powders. So there was but one thing to do, that was trap my intended sitters.

Next night I was ready for them with an ordinary box trap, and even before the appointed time we saw a fine study in black and white come marching around the cow stable with banner-tail aloft, and across the grass toward the kitchen. The box trap was all ready and we--two women including my wife, and half a dozen men of the mountaineer type--were watching. The cat and the dog moved sullenly aside. The Skunk, with the calm confidence of one accustomed to respect, sniffed his way to the box trap with its tempting odorous bait. A Mink or a Marten, not to say a Fox, would have investigated a little before entering. The Skunk indulged in no such waste of time. What had he to fear--he the little lord of all things with the power of smell? He went in like one going home, seized the bait, and down went the door. The uninitiated onlookers expected an explosion from the Skunk, but I knew quite well he never wasted a shot, and did not hesitate to approach and make all safe. Now I wanted to move the box with its captive to my photographic studio, but could not carry it alone, so I asked the mountaineers to come and help. Had I asked them to join me in killing a man, shooting up the town, or otherwise taking their lives in their hands, I would doubtless have had half a dozen cheerful volunteers; but to carry a box in which was a wild Skunk--"not for a hundred dollars," and the warriors melted into the background.

Then I said to my wife, "Haven't you got nerve enough to help with this box? I'll guarantee that nothing will happen." So she came and we took the box to my prepared enclosure, where next day I photographed him to my heart's content. More than once as I worked around at a distance of six or eight feet, the Skunk's tail flew up, but I kept perfectly still then; talked softly, apologizing and explaining: "Now don't shoot at me. We are to be good friends. I wouldn't hurt you for anything. Now do drop that fighting flag, if you please, and be good."

Gradually the tail went down and the captive looked at me in mere curiosity as I got my pictures.

I let him go by simply removing the wire netting of the fence, whereupon he waddled off under the cabin that I called "home."

WE SHARE THE SHANTY WITH THE SKUNKS

The next night as I lay in my bunk I heard a sniffing and scratching on the cabin floor. On looking over the edge of the bed I came face to face with my friend the Skunk. Our noses were but a foot apart and just behind him was another; I suppose his mate. I said: "Hello! Here you are again. I'm glad to see you. Who's your friend?" He did not tell me, neither did he seem offended. I suppose it was his mate. That was the beginning of his residence under the floor of my cabin. My wife and I got very well acquainted with him and his wife before the summer was over. For though we had the cabin by day, the Skunks had it by night. We always left them some scraps, and regularly at dusk they came up to get them. They cleaned up our garbage, so helped to rid us of flies and mice. We were careful to avoid hurting or scaring our nightly visitors, so the summer passed without offense. We formed only the kindest feelings toward each other, and we left them in possession of the cabin, where, so far as I know, they are living yet, if you wish to call.

THE SKUNK AND THE UNWISE BOBCAT

As already noted, I swept the dust smooth around our shanty each night to make a sort of visitors' book. Then each morning I could go out and by study of the tracks get an exact idea of who had called. Of course there were many blank nights; on others the happenings were trifling, but some were full of interest. In this way I learned of the Coyote's visits to the garbage pail and of the Skunk establishment under the house, and other interesting facts as in the diagram. I have always used this method of study in my mountain trips, and recall a most interesting record that rewarded my patience some twenty years ago when I lived in New Mexico.

During the night I had been aroused by a frightful smell of Skunk, followed by strange muffled sounds that died away. So forth I went at sunrise and found the odour of Skunk no dream but a stern reality. Then a consultation of my dust album revealed an inscription which after a little condensing and clearing up appeared much as in Plate XXII. At A a Skunk had come on the scene, at B he was wandering about when a hungry Wild Cat or Bobcat Lynx appeared, C. Noting the promise of something to kill for food, he came on at D. The Skunk observing the intruder said, "You better let me alone." And not wishing to make trouble moved off toward E. But the Bobcat, evidently young and inexperienced, gave chase. At F the Skunk wheeled about, remarking, "Well, if you will have it, here goes!" At G the Lynx was hit. The tremendous bound from G to H shows the effect. At J he bumped into a stone, showing probably that he was blinded, after which he went bouncing and bounding away. The Skunk merely said, "I told you so!" then calmly resumed the even tenor of his way. At K he found the remains of a chicken, on which he feasted, then went quietly home to bed.

This is my reading of the tracks in the dust. The evidence was so clear that I have sketched here from imagination the succession of events which it seemed to narrate.

MY PET SKUNKS

It would not be doing justice to the Skunk if I did not add a word about certain of the kind that I have at home.

For many years I have kept at least one pet Skunk. Just now I have about sixty. I keep them close to the house and would let them run loose indoors but for the possibility of some fool dog or cat coming around, and provoking the exemplary little brutes into a perfectly justifiable endeavour to defend themselves as nature taught them. But for this I should have no fear. Not only do I handle them myself, but I have induced many of my wild-eyed visitors to do so as a necessary part of their education. For few indeed there are in the land to-day that realize the gentleness and forbearance of this righteous little brother of ours, who, though armed with a weapon that will put the biggest and boldest to flight or disastrous defeat, yet refrains from using it until in absolute peril of his life, and then only after several warnings.

By way of rounding out this statement, I present a picture of my little daughter playing among the Skunks, and need add only that they are full-grown specimens in full possession of all their faculties. Plate XXIV.

* * * * *

VII

Old Silver-grizzle--The Badger

* * * * *

VII

Old Silver-grizzle--The Badger

A brilliant newspaper man once gave vast publicity to the story that at last a use had been found for the Badger, with his mania for digging holes in the ground. By kindness and care and the help of an attached little steam-gauge speedometer plumb compass, that gave accurate aim, improved perpendicularity, and increased efficiency to the efforts of the strenuous excavator, he had been able to produce a dirigible Badger that was certain to displace all other machinery for digging postholes.

Unfortunately I was in a position to disprove this pretty conceit. But I think of it every time I put my foot in a Badger hole. Such lovely holes, so plentiful, so worse than useless where the Badger has thoughtlessly located them. If only we could harness and direct such excavatory energies.

This, indeed, is the only quarrel civilized man can pick with the honest Badger. He will dig holes that endanger horse's legs and rider's necks. He may destroy Gophers, Ground-squirrels, Prairie-dogs, insects, and a hundred enemies of the farm; he may help the crops in a thousand different ways, but he will dig post-holes where they are not wanted, and this indiscretion has made many enemies for the kindest and sturdiest of all the squatters on the plains.

THE VALIANT, HARMLESS BADGER

From the Saskatchewan to Mexico he ranges, and from Illinois to California, wherever there are dry, open plains supplied with Ground-squirrels and water.

Many times, in crossing the rolling plains of Montana, the uplands of Arizona and New Mexico, or the prairies of Manitoba, I have met with Mittenusk, as the redmen call him. Like a big white stone perched on some low mound he seems. But the wind makes cracks in it at places, and then it moves--giving plain announcement to the world with eyes to see that this is a Badger sunning himself. He seldom allows a near approach, even in the Yellowstone, where he is safe, and is pretty sure to drop down out of sight in his den long before one gets within camera range. The Badger is such a subterranean, nocturnal creature at most times that for long his home life escaped our observation, but at last a few paragraphs, if not a chapter of it, have been secured, and we find that this shy creature, in ill odour among cattlemen as noted, is a rare and lovely character when permitted to unbend in a congenial group. Sturdy, strong and dogged, and brave to the last ditch, the more we know of the Badger the more we respect him.

Let us pass lightly over the facts that in makeup he is between a Bear and a Weasel, and that he weighs about twenty pounds, and has a soft coat of silvery gray and some label marks of black on his head.

He feeds chiefly on Ground-squirrels, which he digs out, but does not scorn birds' eggs, or even fruit and grain at times. Except for an occasional sun-bath, he spends the day in his den and travels about mostly by night. He minds his own business, if let alone, but woe be to the creature of the plains that tries to molest him, for he has the heart of a bulldog, the claws of a Grizzly, and the jaws of a small crocodile.

I shall never forget my first meeting with Old Silver-grizzle. It was on the plains of the Souris, in 1882. I saw this broad, low, whitish creature on the prairie, not far from the trail, and, impelled by the hunter instinct so strong in all boys, I ran toward him. He dived into a den, but the one he chose proved to be barely three feet deep, and I succeeded in seizing the Badger's short thick tail. Gripping it firmly with both hands, I pulled and pulled, but he was stronger than I. He braced himself against the sides of the den and defied me.

With anything like fair play, he would have escaped, but I had accomplices, and the details of what followed are not pleasant reminiscences. But I was very young at the time, and that was my first Badger. I wanted his skin, and I had not learned to respect his exemplary life and dauntless spirit.

In the summer of 1897 I was staying at Yancey's in the Park. Daily I saw signs of Badgers about, and one morning while prowling, camera in hand, I saw old Gray-coat wandering on the prairie, looking for fresh Ground-squirrel holes. Keeping low, I ran toward him. He soon sensed me, and to my surprise came rushing toward me, uttering sharp snarls. This one was behaving differently from any Badger I had seen before, but evidently he was going to give me a chance for a picture. After that was taken, doubtless I could save myself by running. We were within thirty yards of each other and both coming strong, when "crash" I went into a Badger hole I had not seen, just as he went "thump" down tail first into a hole he had not seen. For a moment we both looked very foolish, but he recovered first, and rushing a few yards nearer, plunged into a deep and wide den toward which he evidently had been heading from the first.

HIS SOCIABLE BENT

The strongest peculiar trait of the Badger is perhaps his sociability-- sociability being, of course, a very different thing from gregariousness. Usually there are two Badgers in each den. Nothing peculiar about that, but there are several cases on record of a Badger, presumably a bachelor or a widower, sharing his life with some totally different animal. In some instances that other animal has been a Coyote; and the friendship really had its foundation in enmity and intended robbery.

This is the probable history of a typical case: The Badger, being a mighty miner and very able to dig out the Ground-squirrels of the prairie, was followed about by a Coyote, whose speed and agility kept him safe from the Badger's jaws, while he hovered close by, knowing quite well that when the Badger was digging out the Ground-squirrels at their front door, these rodents were very apt to bolt by the back door, and thus give the Coyote an excellent chance for a cheap dinner.

So the Coyote acquired the habit of following the hard-working Badger. At first, no doubt, the latter resented the parasite that dogged his steps, but becoming used to it "first endured, then pitied, then embraced", or, to put it more mildly, he got accustomed to the Coyote's presence, and being of a kindly disposition, forgot his enmity and thenceforth they contentedly lived their lives together. I do not know that they inhabited the same den. Yet that would not be impossible, since similar things are reported of the British Badger and the Fox.

More than one observer has seen a Badger and a Coyote travelling together, sometimes one leading, sometimes the other. Evidently it was a partnership founded on good-will, however it may have been begun.

THE STORY OF THE KINDLY BADGER

But the most interesting case, and one which I might hesitate to reproduce but for the witnesses, reached me at Winnipeg.

In 1871 there was a family named Service living at Bird's Hill, on the prairie north of Winnipeg. They had one child, a seven-year-old boy named Harry. He was a strange child, very small for his age, and shy without being cowardly. He had an odd habit of following dogs, chickens, pigs, and birds, imitating their voices and actions, with an exactness that onlookers sometimes declared to be uncanny. One day he had gone quietly after a Prairie Chicken that kept moving away from him without taking flight, clucking when she clucked, and nodding his head or shaking his "wings" when she did. So he wandered on and on, till the house was hidden from view behind the trees that fringed the river, and the child was completely lost.

There was nothing remarkable in his being away for several hours, but a heavy thunderstorm coming up that afternoon called attention to the fact that the boy was missing, and when the first casual glance did not discover him it became serious and a careful search was begun.

Father and mother, with the near neighbours, scoured the prairie till dark, and began the next day at dawn, riding in all directions, calling, and looking for signs. After a day or two the neighbours gave it up, believing that the child was drowned and carried away by the river. But the parents continued their search even long after all hope seemed dead. And there was no hour of the day when that stricken mother did not send up a prayer for heavenly help; nor any night when she did not kneel with her husband and implore the One who loved and blessed the babes of Jerusalem to guard her little one and bring him back in safety.

THE EVIL ONE

There was one neighbour of the family who joined in the search that had nevertheless incurred the bitter dislike of little Harry Service. The feeling was partly a mere baby instinct, but pointedly because of the man's vicious cruelty to the animals, wild or tame, that came within his power. Only a week before he had set steel traps at a den where he chanced to find a pair of Badgers in residence. The first night he captured the father Badger. The cruel jaws of the jag-toothed trap had seized him by both paws, so he was held helpless. The trap was champed and wet with blood and froth when Grogan came in the morning. Of what use are courage and strength when one cannot reach the foe? The Badger craved only a fair fight, but Grogan stood out of reach and used a club till the light was gone from the brave eyes and the fighting snarl was still.

The trap was reset in the sand and Grogan went. He carried the dead Badger to the Service house to show his prize and get help to skin it, after which he set off for the town and bartered the skin for what evil indulgence it might command, and thought no more of the trap for three days. Meanwhile the mother Badger, coming home at dawn, was caught by one foot. Strain as she might, that deadly grip still held her; all that night and all the next day she struggled. She had little ones to care for. Their hungry cries from down the burrow were driving her almost mad; but the trap was of strong steel, beyond her strength, and at last the crying of the little ones in the den grew still. On the second day of her torture the mother, in desperation, chewed off one of her toes and dragged her bleeding foot from the trap.

Down the burrow she went first, but it was too late; her babies were dead. She buried them where they lay and hastened from that evil spot.

Water was her first need, next food, and then at evening she made for an old den she had used the fall before.

THE BADGER THAT RESCUED THE BOY

And little Harry, meanwhile, where was he? That sunny afternoon in June he had wandered away from the house, and losing sight of the familiar building behind the long fringe of trees by the river, he had lost his bearings. Then came the thunder shower which made him seek for shelter. There was nothing about him but level prairie, and the only shelter he could find was a Badger hole, none too wide even for his small form. Into this he had backed and stayed with some comfort during the thunderstorm, which continued till night. Then in the evening the child heard a sniffing sound, and a great, gray animal loomed up against the sky, sniffed at the tracks and at the open door of the den. Next it put its head in, and Harry saw by the black marks on its face that it was a Badger. He had seen one just three days before. A neighbour had brought it to his father's house to skin it. There it stood sniffing, and Harry, gazing with less fear than most children, noticed that the visitor had five claws on one foot and four on the other, with recent wounds, proof of some sad experience in a trap. Doubtless this was the Badger's den, for she--it proved a mother--came in, but Harry had no mind to surrender. The Badger snarled and came on, and Harry shrieked, "Get out!" and struck with his tiny fists, and then, to use his own words, "I scratched the Badger's face and she scratched mine." Surely this Badger was in a generous mood, for she did him no serious harm, and though the rightful owner of the den, she went away and doubtless slept elsewhere.

Night came down. Harry was very thirsty. Close by the door was a pool of rainwater. He crawled out, slaked his thirst, and backed into the warm den as far as he could. Then remembering his prayers, he begged God to "send mamma," and cried himself to sleep. During the night he was awakened by the Badger coming again, but it went away when the child scolded it. Next morning Harry went to the pool again and drank. Now he was so hungry; a few old rose hips hung on the bushes near the den. He gathered and ate these, but was even hungrier. Then he saw something moving out on the plain. It might be the Badger, so he backed into the den, but he watched the moving thing. It was a horseman galloping. As it came near, Harry saw that it was Grogan, the neighbour for whom he had such a dislike, so he got down out of sight. Twice that morning men came riding by, but having once yielded to his shy impulse, he hid again each time. The Badger came back at noon. In her mouth she held the body of a Prairie Chicken, pretty well plucked and partly devoured. She came into the den sniffing as before. Harry shouted, "Get out! Go away." The Badger dropped the meat and raised her head. Harry reached and grasped the food and devoured it with the appetite of one starving. There must have been another doorway, for later the Badger was behind the child in the den, and still later when he had fallen asleep she came and slept beside him. He awoke to find the warm furry body filling the space between him and the wall, and knew now why it was he had slept so comfortably.

That evening the Badger brought the egg of a Prairie Chicken and set it down unbroken before the child. He devoured it eagerly, and again drank from the drying mud puddle to quench his thirst. During the night it rained again, and he would have been cold, but the Badger came and cuddled around him. Once or twice it licked his face. The child could not know, but the parents discovered later that this was a mother Badger which had lost her brood and her heart was yearning for something to love.

Now there were two habits that grew on the boy. One was to shun the men that daily passed by in their search, the other was to look to the Badger for food and protection, and live the Badger's life. She brought him food often not at all to his taste--dead Mice or Ground-squirrels--but several times she brought in the comb of a bee's nest or eggs of game birds, and once a piece of bread almost certainly dropped on the trail from some traveller's lunch bag. His chief trouble was water. The prairie pool was down to mere ooze and with this he moistened his lips and tongue. Possibly the mother Badger wondered why he did not accept her motherly offerings. But rain came often enough to keep him from serious suffering.

Their daily life was together now, and with the imitative power strong in all children and dominant in him, he copied the Badger's growls, snarls, and purrs. Sometimes they played tag on the prairie, but both were ready to rush below at the slightest sign of a stranger.

Two weeks went by. Galloping men no longer passed each day. Harry and the Badger had fitted their lives into each other's, and strange as it may seem, the memory of his home was already blurred and weakened in the boy. Once or twice during the second week men had passed near by, but the habit of eluding them was now in full possession of him.

FINDING THE LOST ONE

One morning he wandered a little farther in search of water and was alarmed by a horseman appearing. He made for home on all fours--he ran much on all fours now--and backed into the den. In the prairie grass he was concealed, but the den was on a bare mound, and the horseman caught a glimpse of a whitish thing disappearing down the hole. Badgers were familiar to him, but the peculiar yellow of this and the absence of black marks gave it a strange appearance. He rode up quietly within twenty yards and waited.

After a few minutes the gray-yellow ball slowly reappeared and resolved itself into the head of a tow-topped child. The young man leaped to the ground and rushed forward, but the child retreated far back into the den, beyond reach of the man, and refused to come out. Nevertheless, there was no doubt that this was the missing Harry Service. "Harry! Harry! don't you know me? I'm your Cousin Jack," the young man said in soothing, coaxing tones. "Harry, won't you come out and let me take you back to mamma? Come Harry! Look! here are some cookies!" but all in vain. The child hissed and snarled at him like a wild thing, and retreated as far as he could till checked by a turn in the burrow.

Now Jack got out his knife and began to dig until the burrow was large enough for him to crawl in a little way. At once he succeeded in getting hold of the little one's arm and drew him out struggling and crying. But now there rushed also from the hole a Badger, snarling and angry; it charged at the man, uttering its fighting snort. He fought it off with his whip, then swung to the saddle with his precious burden and rode away as for his very life, while the Badger pursued for a time, but it was easily left behind, and its snorts were lost and forgotten.

HOME AGAIN

The father was coming in from another direction as he saw this strange sight: a horse galloping madly over the prairie, on its back a young man shouting loudly, and in his arms a small dirty child, alternately snarling at his captor, trying to scratch his face, or struggling to be free.

The father was used to changing intensity of feeling at these times, but he turned pale and held his breath till the words reached him: "I have got him, thank God! He's all right," and he rushed forward shouting, "My boy! my boy!"

But he got a rude rebuff. The child glared like a hunted cat, hissed at him, and menaced with hands held claw fashion. Fear and hate were all he seemed to express. The door of the house was flung open and the distracted mother, now suddenly overjoyed, rushed to join the group. "My darling! my darling!" she sobbed, but little Harry was not as when he left them. He hung back, he hid his face in the coat of his captor, he scratched and snarled like a beast, he displayed his claws and threatened fight, till strong arms gathered him up and placed him on his mother's knees in the old, familiar room with the pictures, and the clock ticking as of old, and the smell of frying bacon, his sister's voice, and his father's form, and, above all, his mother's arms about him, her magic touch on his brow, and her voice, "My darling! my darling! Oh! Harry, don't you know your mother? My boy! my boy!" And the struggling little wild thing in her arms grew quiet, his animal anger died away, his raucous hissing gave place to a short panting, and that to a low sobbing that ended in a flood of tears and a passionate "Mamma, mamma, mamma!" as the veil of a different life was rolled away, and he clung to his mother's bosom.

But even as she cooed to him, and stroked his brow and won him back again, there was a strange sound, a snarling hiss at the open door. All turned to see a great Badger standing there with its front feet on the threshold. Father and cousin exclaimed, "Look at that Badger!" and reached for the ready gun, but the boy screamed again. He wriggled from his mother's arms and rushing to the door, cried, "My Badgie! my Badgie!" He flung his arms about the savage thing's neck, and it answered with a low purring sound as it licked its lost companion's face. The men were for killing the Badger, but it was the mother's keener insight that saved it, as one might save a noble dog that had rescued a child from the water.

It was some days before the child would let the father come near. "I hate that man; he passed me every day and would not look at me," was the only explanation. Doubtless the first part was true, for the Badger den was but two miles from the house and the father rode past many times in his radiating search, but the tow-topped head had escaped his eye.

It was long and only by slow degrees that the mother got the story that is written here, and parts of it were far from clear. It might all have been dismissed as a dream or a delirium but for the fact that the boy had been absent two weeks; he was well and strong now, excepting that his lips were blackened and cracked with the muddy water, the Badger had followed him home, and was now his constant friend.

It was strange to see how the child oscillated between the two lives, sometimes talking to his people exactly as he used to talk, and sometimes running on all fours, growling, hissing, and tussling with the Badger. Many a game of "King of the Castle" they had together on the low pile of sand left after the digging of a new well. Each would climb to the top and defy the other to pull him down, till a hold was secured and they rolled together to the level, clutching and tugging, Harry giggling, the Badger uttering a peculiar high-pitched sound that might have been called snarling had it not been an expression of good nature. Surely it was a Badger laugh. There was little that Harry could ask without receiving, in those days, but his mother was shocked when he persisted that the Badger must sleep in his bed; yet she so arranged it. The mother would go in the late hours and look on them with a little pang of jealousy as she saw her baby curled up, sleeping soundly with that strange beast.

It was Harry's turn to feed his friend now, and side by side they sat to eat. The Badger had become an established member of the family. But after a month had gone by an incident took place that I would gladly leave untold.

THE HUMAN BRUTE

Grogan, the unpleasant neighbour, who had first frightened Harry into the den, came riding up to the Service homestead. Harry was in the house for the moment. The Badger was on the sand pile. Instantly on catching sight of it, Grogan unslung his gun and exclaimed, "A Badger!" To him a Badger was merely something to be killed. "Bang!" and the kindly animal rolled over, stung and bleeding, but recovered and dragged herself toward the house. "Bang!" and the murderer fired again, just as the inmates rushed to the door- -too late. Harry ran toward the Badger shouting, "Badgie! my Badgie!" He flung his baby arms around the bleeding neck. It fawned on him feebly, purring a low, hissing purr, then mixing the purrs with moans, grew silent, and slowly sank down, and died in his arms. "My Badgie! my Badgie!" the boy wailed, and all the ferocity of his animal nature was directed against Grogan.

"You better get out of this before I kill you!" thundered the father, and the hulking halfbreed sullenly mounted his horse and rode away.

A great part of his life had been cut away and it seemed as though a deathblow had been dealt the boy. The shock was more than he could stand. He moaned and wept all day, he screamed himself into convulsions, he was worn out at sundown and slept little that night. Next morning he was in a raging fever and ever he called for "My Badgie!" He seemed at death's door the next day, but a week later he began to mend and in three weeks was strong as ever and childishly gay, with occasional spells of sad remembering that gradually ceased.

He grew up to early manhood in a land of hunters, but he took no pleasure in the killing that was such sport to his neighbour's sons, and to his dying day he could not look on the skin of a Badger without feelings of love, tenderness, and regret.

This is the story of the Badger as it was told me, and those who wish to inquire further can do so at Winnipeg, if they seek out Archbishop Matheson, Dr. R. M. Simpson, or Mrs. George A. Frazer of Kildonan. These witnesses may differ as to the details, but all have assured me that in its main outlines this tale is true, and I gladly tell it, for I want you to realize the kindly disposition that is in that sturdy, harmless, noble wild animal that sits on the low prairie mounds, for then I know that you will join with me in loving him, and in seeking to save his race from extermination.

* * * * *

VIII

The Squirrel and His Jerky-tail Brothers

* * * * *

The Squirrel and His Jerky-tail Brothers

You remember that Hiawatha christened the Squirrel "Adjidaumo"--"Tail-in-air" and this Tail-in-air was chattering overhead as I sat, some twenty-five years ago, on the shore of the Lake of the Woods with an Ojibwa Indian, checking up the animals' names in the native tongue. Of course the Red-squirrel was early in our notice.

"Ad-je-daw-mo" I called it, but the Indian corrected me; "Ah-chit-aw-mo" he made it; and when I translated it "Tail-in-air" he said gravely, "No, it means head downward." Then noting my surprise, he added, with characteristic courtesy, "Yes, yes, you are right; if his head is down, his tail must be up." Thoreau talks of the Red-squirrel flicking his tail like a whip-lash, and the word "Squirrel," from the Latin "Sciurus" and Greek "Skia-oura" means "shady tail." Thus all of its names seem to note the wonderful banner that serves the animal in turn as sun-shade, signal-flag, coverlet, and parachute.

THE CHEEKY PINE SQUIRREL

A wonderfully extensive kingdom has fallen to Adjidaumo of the shady tail; all of Canada and most of the Rockies are his. He is at home wherever there are pine forests and a cool climate; and he covers so many ranges of diverse conditions that, responding to the new environments in lesser matters of makeup, we have a score of different Squirrel races from this parent stock. In size, in tail, in kind or depth of coat they differ to the expert eye, but so far as I can see they are exactly alike in all their ways, their calls and their dispositions.

The Pine Squirrel is the form found in the Rockies about the Yellowstone Park. It is a little darker in colour than the Red-squirrel of the East, but I find no other difference. It has the same aggressive, scolding propensities, the same love of the pinyons and their product, the same friends and the same foes, with one possible partial exception in the list of habits, and that is in its method of storing up mushrooms.

The pinyons, or nuts of the pinyon pine, are perhaps the most delicious nuts in all the lap of bountiful dame Nature, from fir belt in the north to equatorial heat and on to far Fuego. All wild creatures revel in the pinyons. To the Squirrels they are more than the staff of life; they are meat and potatoes, bread and honey, pork and beans, bread and cake, sugar and chocolate, the sum of comfort, and the promise of continuing joy. But the pinyon does not bear every year; there are off years, as with other trees, and the Squirrels might be in a bad way if they had no other supply of food to lay up for the winter.

A season I spent in the Southern Rockies was an off year for pinyons, and when September came I was shown what the Squirrels do in such an emergency. All through autumn the slopes of the hills were dotted with the umbrellas of countless toadstools or mushrooms, representing many fat and wholesome species. It is well known that while a few of them are poisonous, a great many are good food. Scientists can find out which is which only by slow experiment. "Eat them; if you live they are good, if you die they are poisonous" has been suggested as a certain method. The Squirrels must have worked this out long ago, for they surely know the good ones; and all through late summer they are at work gathering them for winter use in place of the pine-nuts.

Now if the provident Squirrel stored these up as he does the pinyons, in holes or underground, they would surely go to mush in a short time and be lost. He makes no such mistake. He stores them in the forked branches of trees, where they dry out and remain good until needed; and wisely puts them high enough up to be out of reach of the Deer and low enough to avoid being dislodged by the wind.

As you ramble through the Squirrel-frequented woods, you will often come across a log or stump which is littered over with the scales fresh cut from a pine cone; sometimes there is a pile of a bushel or more by the place; you have stumbled on a Squirrel's workshop. Here is where he does his husking, and the "clear corn" produced is stored away in some underground granary till It is needed.

The Pine Squirrel loves to nest in a hollow tree, but also builds an outside nest which at a distance looks like a mass of rubbish. This, on investigation, turns out to be a convenient warm chamber some six inches wide and two or three high. It is covered with a waterproof roof of bark thatch, and entered by a door artfully concealed with layers and fringes of bark that hide it alike from blood-thirsty foes and piercing winter blasts.

CHIPMUNKS AND GROUND-SQUIRRELS

The Red-squirrel is safe and happy only when in the tall trees, but his kinsmen have sought out any and every different environment. One enormous group of his great grandfather's second cousins have abandoned tree life altogether. They have settled down like the Dakota farmers, to be happy on the prairie, where, never having need to get over anything higher than their own front doorstep, they have lost the last vestige of power to climb. These are the Ground-squirrels, that in a variety of forms are a pest in gardens and on farms in most of the country west of the Mississippi.

Standing between these and the true Squirrels are the elegant Chipmunks, the prettiest and most popular of all the family. They frequent the borderland between woods and prairie; they climb, if anything is to be gained by it, but they know, like the Ground-squirrels, that Mother Earth is a safer retreat in time of danger than the tallest tree that ever grew.

THE GROUND-SQUIRREL THAT PLAYS PICKET-PIN

Conspicuous in its teeming numbers in the Yellowstone Park is the Picket-Pin Ground-squirrel. On every level, dry prairie along the great river I found it in swarms.

It looks much like a common Squirrel, but its coat has become more mud-coloured, and its tail is reduced by long ages of neglect to a mere vestige of the ancestral banner. It has developed great powers of burrowing, but it never climbs anything higher than the little mound that it makes about the door of its home.

The Picket-pin is an interesting and picturesque creature in some ways, but it has one habit that I cannot quite condone. In this land of sun and bright blue air, this world of outdoor charm, it comes forth tardily in late spring, as late sometimes as the first of May, and promptly retires in mid-August, when blazing summer is on the face of the earth, and the land is a land of plenty. Down it goes after three and one half short months, to sleep for eight and a half long ones; and since during these three and a half months it is above ground only in broad daylight, this means that for only two months of the year it is active, and the other ten, four fifths of its life, it passes in a deathlike sleep.

Of course, the Picket-pin might reply that it has probably as many hours of active life as any of its kind, only it breaks them up into sections, with long blanks of rest between. Whether this defense is a good one or not, we have no facts at present to determine.

It has a fashion of sitting up straight on the doorway mound when it wishes to take an observation, and the more it is alarmed by the approach of an enemy the straighter it sits up, pressing its paws tight to its ribs, so that at a short distance it looks like a picket-pin of wood; hence the name.

Oftentimes some tenderfoot going in the evening to stake out his horse and making toward the selected patch of grassy prairie, exclaims, "Good Luck! here's a picket-pin already driven in." But on leading up his horse within ten or twelve feet of the pin, it gives a little "chirr" and dives down out of sight. Then the said tenderfoot realizes why the creature got the name.

The summer of 1897 I spent in the Park about Yancey's and there had daily chances of seeing the Picket-pin and learning its ways, for the species was there in thousands on the little prairie about my cabin. I think I am safe in saying that there were ten families to the acre of land on all the level prairie in this valley.

CHINK AND THE PICKET-PINS

As already noted in the Coyote chapter, we had in camp that summer the little dog called Chink. He was just old enough to think himself a remarkable dog with a future before him. There was hardly anything that Chink would not attempt, except perhaps keeping still. He was always trying to do some absurd and impossible thing, or, if he did attempt the possible, he usually spoiled his best efforts by his way of going about it. He once spent a whole morning trying to run up a tall, straight, pine tree in whose branches was a snickering Pine Squirrel.

The darling ambition of his life for some weeks was to catch one of the Picket-pin Ground-squirrels that swarmed on the prairie about the camp.

Chink had determined to catch one of these Ground-squirrels the very first day he came into the valley. Of course, he went about it in his own original way, doing everything wrong end first, as usual. This, his master said, was due to a streak of Irish in his makeup. So Chink would begin a most elaborate stalk a quarter of a mile from the Ground-squirrel. After crawling on his breast from tussock to tussock for a hundred yards or so, the nervous strain would become too great, and Chink, getting too much excited to crawl, would rise on his feet and walk straight toward the Squirrel, which would now be sitting up by its hole, fully alive to the situation.

After a minute or two of this very open approach, Chink's excitement would overpower all caution. He would begin running, and at the last, just as he should have done his finest stalking, he would go bounding and barking toward the Ground-squirrel, which would sit like a peg of wood till the proper moment, then dive below with a derisive chirrup, throwing with its hind feet a lot of sand right into Chink's eager, open mouth.

Day after day this went on with level sameness, and still Chink did not give up, although I feel sure he had bushels of sand thrown in his mouth that summer by the impudent Picket-pins.

Perseverance, he seemed to believe, must surely win in the end, as indeed it did. For, one day, he made an unusually elaborate stalk after an unusually fine big Picket-pin, carried out all his absurd tactics, finishing with the grand, boisterous charge, and actually caught his victim; but this time it happened to be a wooden picket-pin. Any one who doubts that a dog knows when he has made a fool of himself should have seen Chink that day as he sheepishly sneaked out of sight behind the tent.

CHIPMUNKS

Every one recognizes as a Chipmunk the lively little creature that, with striped coat and with tail aloft, dashes across all the roads and chirrups on all the log piles that line the roads throughout the timbered portions of the Park. I am sure I have often seen a thousand of them in a mile of road between the Mammoth Hot Springs and Norris Geyser Basin. The traveller who makes the entire round of the Park may see a hundred thousand if he keeps his eyes open. While every one knows them at once for Chipmunks, it takes a second and more careful glance to show they are of three totally distinct kinds.

THE GROUND-SQUIRREL THAT PRETENDS IT'S A CHIPMUNK

First, largest, and least common, is the Big Striped Ground-squirrel, the Golden Ground-squirrel or Say's Ground-squirrel, called scientifically Citellus lateralis cinerascens. This, in spite of its livery, is not a Chipmunk at all but a Ground-squirrel that is trying hard to be a Chipmunk. And it makes a good showing so far as manners, coat and stripes are concerned, but the incontrovertible evidence of its inner life, as indicated by skull and makeup, tells us plainly that it is merely a Ground-squirrel, a first cousin to the ignoble Picket-pin.

I found it especially common in the higher parts of the Park. It is really a mountain species, at home chiefly among the rocks, yet is very ready to take up its abode under buildings. At the Lake Hotel I saw a number of them that lived around the back door, and were almost tamed through the long protection there given them. Like most of these small rodents, they are supposed to be grain-eaters but they really are omnivorous, and quite ready to eat flesh and eggs, as well as seeds and fruit. Warren in his "Mammals of Colorado," tells of having seen one of these Ground-squirrels kill some young Bluebirds; and adds another instance of flesh-eating observed in the Yellowstone Park, where he and two friends, riding along one of the roads, saw a Say Ground-squirrel demurely squatting on a log, holding in its arms a tiny young Meadow Mouse, from which it picked the flesh as one might pick corn from a cob. Meadow Mice are generally considered a nuisance, and the one devoured probably was of a cantankerous disposition; but just the same it gives one an unpleasant sensation to think of this elegant little creature, in appearance, innocence personified, wearing all the insignia of a grain-eater, yet ruthlessly indulging in such a bloody and cannibal feast.

A FOUR-LEGGED BIRD--THE NORTHERN CHIPMUNK

The early naturalists who first made the acquaintance of the Eastern Ground-squirrel named it Tamias or "The Steward." Later the Northern Chipmunk was discovered and it was found to be more of a Chipmunk than its Eastern cousin. The new one had all the specialties of the old kind, but in a higher degree. So they named this one Eutamias, which means "good" or "extra good" Chipmunk. And extra good this exquisite little creature surely is in all that goes to make a charming, graceful, birdy, pert and vivacious four-foot. In everything but colours it is Eutamias or Tamias of a more intensified type. Its tail is long in proportion and carried differently, being commonly held straight up, so that the general impression one gets is of a huge tail with a tiny striped animal attached to its lower end.

Its excessive numbers along the roads in the Park are due to two things: First, the food, for oats are continually spilled from the freighting wagons. Second, the protection of piles of pine trees cut and cast aside in clearing the roadway.

There is one habit of the Eastern Chipmunk that I have not noted in the mountain species, and that is the habit of song. In the early spring and late autumn when the days are bright and invigorating, the Eastern Chipmunk will mount some log, stump or other perch and express his exuberant joy in a song which is a rapid repetition of a bird-like note suggested by "Chuck," "Chuck," or "Chock," "Chock." This is kept up two or three minutes without interruption, and is one of those delightful woodland songs whose charm comes rather from association than from its inherent music.

If our Western Chipmunk is as far ahead in matters musical as he is in form and other habits, I shall expect him to render no less than the song of a nightingale when he gives himself up to express his wild exuberance in a chant.

I shall never forget the days I spent with a naturalist friend in an old mill building in western Manitoba. It was in a pine woods which was peopled with these little Chipmunks. They had hailed the mill and its wood piles, and especially the stables, with their squandered oats, as the very gifts of a beneficient Providence for their use and benefit. They had concentrated on the mill; they were there in hundreds, almost thousands, and whenever one looked across the yard in sunny hours one could see a dozen or more together.

The old mill was infested with them as an old brewery with rats. But in many respects besides beauty they were an improvement on rats: they did not smell, they were not vicious, and they did not move by night.

During the daytime they were everywhere and into everything. Our slender stock of provisions was badly reduced when, by mischance, the tin box was left open a few hours, but we loved to see so much beautiful life about and so forgave them. One of our regular pleasures was to sit back after a meal and watch these pert-eyed, four-legged birds scramble onto the table, eat the scraps and lick all the plates and platters clean.

Like all the Chipmunks and Ground-squirrels, this animal has well-developed cheek-pouches which it uses for carrying home seeds and roots which serve for food in the winter. Or perhaps we should say in the early spring, for the Chipmunk, like the Ground-squirrel, goes into the ground for a long repose as soon as winter comes down hard and white.

Yet it does not go so early or stay so late as its big cousin. October still sees it active, even running about in the snow. As late as October 31st at Breckenridge, Col., I saw one sitting up on a log and eating some grass or seeds during a driving snowstorm. High up in the Shoshonees, after winter had settled down, on October 8, 1898, I saw one of these bright creatures bounding through the snow. On a stone he paused to watch me and I made a hasty sketch of his attitude.

Then, again, it is out in the spring, early in April, so that it is above ground for at least seven months of the year. Its nest is in a chamber at the end of a long tunnel that it digs under ground, usually among roots that make hard digging for the creatures that would rout them out. Very little is known as yet, however, about the growth or development of the young, so here is an opportunity for the young naturalist who would contribute something to our knowledge of this interesting creature.

A STRIPED PIGMY--THE LEAST CHIPMUNK

Closely akin to this one and commonly mistaken for its young, is the Least Chipmunk (Eutamias minimus), which is widely diffused in the great dry central region of the Continent. Although so generally found and so visible when found, its history is practically unknown. It probably lives much like its relatives, raising a brood of four to six young in a warm chamber far underground, and brings them up to eat all manner of seeds, grains, fruits, herbs, berries, insects, birds, eggs, and even mice, just as do most of its kinsmen, but no one has proved any of these things. Any exact observations you may make are sure to be acceptable contributions to science.

* * * * *

IX

The Rabbits and their Habits

* * * * *

IX

The Rabbits and their Habits

If the Wolf may be justly proud of his jaws and the Antelope of his legs, I am sure that the Rabbit should very properly glory in his matchless fecundity. To perfect this power he has consecrated all the splendid energies of his vigorous frame, and he has magnified his specialty into a success that is worth more to his race than could be any other single gift.

Rabbits are without weapons of defense, and are simple-minded to the last degree. Most are incapable of long-distance speed, but all have an exuberance of multiplication that fills their ranks as fast as foe can thin the line. If, indeed, they did not have several families, several times a year, they would have died out several epochs back.

There are three marked types of Rabbits in the Rockies--the Cottontail, the Snowshoe, and the Jackrabbit. All of them are represented on the Yellowstone, besides the little Coney of the rocks which is a remote second cousin of the family.

MOLLY COTTONTAIL, THE CLEVER FREEZER

I have often had occasion to comment on the "freezing" of animals. When they are suddenly aware of a near enemy or confronted by unexpected situations, their habit is to freeze--that is, become perfectly rigid, and remain so until the danger is past or at least comprehended.

Molly Cottontail is one of the best "freezers." Whenever she does not know what to do, she does nothing, obeying the old Western rule, "Never rush when you are rattled." Now Molly is a very nervous creature. Any loud, sharp noise is liable to upset her, and feeling herself unnerved she is very apt to stop and simply "freeze." Keep this in mind when next you meet a Cottontail, and get a photograph.

In July, 1902, I tried it myself. I was camped with a lot of Sioux Indians on the banks of the Cheyenne River in Dakota. They had their families with them, and about sundown one of the boys ran into the tepee for a gun, and then fired into the grass. His little brother gave a war-whoop that their "pa" might well have been proud of, then rushed forward and held up a fat Cottontail, kicking her last kick. Another, a smaller Cottontail, was found not far away, and half a dozen young redskins armed with sticks crawled up, then suddenly let them fly. Bunny was hit, knocked over, and before he could recover, a dog had him.

I had been some distance away. On hearing the uproar I came back toward my own campfire, and as I did so, my Indian guide pointed to a Cottontail twenty feet away gazing toward the boys. The guide picked up a stick of firewood.

The boys saw him, and knowing that another Rabbit was there they came running. Now I thought they had enough game for supper and did not wish them to kill poor Molly. But I knew I could not stop them by saying that, so I said: "Hold on till I make a photo." Some of them understood; at any rate, my guide did, and all held back as I crawled toward the Rabbit. She took alarm and was bounding away when I gave a shrill whistle which turned her into a "frozen" statue. Then I came near and snapped the camera. The Indian boys now closed in and were going to throw, but I cried out: "Hold on! not yet; I want another." So I chased Bunny twenty or thirty yards, then gave another shrill whistle, and got a fourth snap. Again I had to hold the boys back by "wanting another picture." Five times I did this, taking five pictures, and all the while steering Molly toward a great pile of drift logs by the river. I had now used up all my films.

The boys were getting impatient. So I addressed the Cottontail solemnly and gently: "Bunny, I have done my best for you. I cannot hold these little savages any longer. You see that pile of logs over there? Well, Bunny, you have just five seconds to get into that wood-pile. Now git!" and I shooed and clapped my hands, and all the young Indians yelled and hurled their clubs, the dogs came bounding and Molly fairly dusted the earth.

"Go it, Molly!"

"Go it, dogs!"

"Ki-yi, Injuns!"

The clubs flew and rattled around her, but Molly put in ten feet to the hop and ten hops to the second (almost), and before the chase was well begun it was over; her cotton tuft disappeared under a log; she was safe in the pile of wood, where so far as I know she lived happy ever after.

THE RABBIT THAT WEARS SNOWSHOES

The Snowshoe Rabbit is found in all parts of the Park, though not in very great numbers. It is called "Snowshoe" on account of the size of its feet, which, already large, are in snow time made larger by fringes of stiff bristles that give the creature such a broad area of support that it can skip on the surface of soft snow while all its kinsmen sink in helplessness.

Here is the hind foot of a Snowshoe in winter, contrasted with the hind foot of a Jackrabbit that was nearly three times its weight.

Rabbits are low in the scale of intelligence, but they are high enough to have some joy in social life. It always gives one a special thrill of satisfaction when favoured with a little glimpse into the home ways, the games, or social life of an animal; and the peep I had into the Rabbit world one night, though but a small affair, I have always remembered with pleasure, and hope for a second similar chance.

This took place in the Bitterroot Mountains in Idaho, in 1902. My wife and I were out on a pack-train trip with two New York friends. We had seen some rough country in Colorado and Wyoming, but we soon agreed that the Bitterroots were the roughest of all the mountains. It took twenty-eight horses to carry the stuff, for which eighteen were enough in the more southern Rockies.

The trails were so crooked and hidden in thick woods, that sometimes the man at the rear might ride the whole day, and never see all the horses until we stopped again for the night.

THE TERROR OF THE MOUNTAIN TRAILS

There were other annoyances, and among them a particularly dangerous animal. The country was fairly stocked with Moose, Elk, Blacktail, Sheep, Goats, Badgers, Skunks, Wolverines, Foxes, Coyotes, Mountain Lions, Lynx, Wolves, Black Bears and Grizzly Bears, but it was none of these that inspired us with fear. The deadly, dangerous creature, the worst of all, was the common Yellow-Jacket-Wasp. These Wasps abounded in the region. Their nests were so plentiful that many were on, or by, the narrow crooked trails that we must follow. Generally these trails were along the mountain shoulder with a steep bank on the upside, and a sheer drop on the other. It was at just such dangerous places that we seemed most often to find the Yellow-Jackets at home. Roused by the noise and trampling, they would assail the horses in swarms, and then there would be a stampede of bucking, squealing, tortured animals. Some would be forced off the trail, and, as has often happened elsewhere, dashed to their death below. This was the daily danger.

One morning late in September we left camp about eight, and set off in the usual line, the chief guide leading and the rest of us distributed at intervals among the pack-horses, as a control. Near the rear was the cook, after him a pack-horse with tins and dishes, and last of all myself.

At first we saw no wasps, as the morning was frosty, but about ten the sun had become strong, the air was quite mild, and the wasps became lively. For all at once I heard the dreaded cry, "Yellow-Jackets!" Then in a moment it was taken up by the cook just ahead of me. "Yellow-Jackets! look out!" with a note almost of terror in his voice.

At once his horse began to plunge and buck. I saw the man of pots clinging to the saddle and protecting his face as best he could, while his mount charged into the bushes and disappeared.

Then "bzz-z-z-z" they went at the pot-horse and again the bucking and squealing, with pots going clank, clink, rattle and away.

"Bzz-z-z-z-z" and in a moment the dark and raging little terrors came at me in a cloud. I had no time to stop, or get off, or seek another way. So I jerked up a coat collar to save my face, held my head low, and tried to hold on, while the little pony went insane with the fiery baptism now upon him. Plunging, kicking, and squealing he went, and I stuck, to him for one--two--three jumps, but at number four, as I remember it, I went flying over his head, fortunately up hill, and landed in the bushes unhurt, but ready for peace at any price.

It is good old wisdom to "lay low in case of doubt," and very low I lay there, waiting for the war to cease. It was over in a few seconds, for my horse dashed after his fellows and passed through the bushes, so that the winged scorpions were left behind. Presently I lifted my head and looked cautiously toward the wasp's-nest. It was in a bank twenty feet away, and the angry swarm was hovering over it, like smoke from a vent hole. They were too angry, and I was too near, to run any risks, so I sank down again and waited. In one or two minutes I peered once more, getting a sight under a small log lying eight or ten feet away. And as I gazed waspward my eye also took in a brown furry creature calmly sitting under the log, wabbling his nose at me and the world about him. It was a young Snowshoe Rabbit.

BUNNY'S RIDE

There is a certain wild hunter instinct in us all, a wish to capture every wood creature we meet. That impulse came on me in power. There was no more danger from wasps, so I got cautiously above this log, put a hand down at each side, grabbed underneath, and the Rabbit was my prisoner. Now I had him, what was I going to do with him--kill him? Certainly not. I began to talk to him. "Now what did I catch you for?" His only reply was a wobble of his nose, so I continued: "I didn't know when I began, but I know now. I want to get your picture." And again the nose wobbled.

I could not take it then as my camera had gone on with my horse. I had nothing to put the Rabbit in. I could not put it in my pocket as that would mean crushing it in some early tumble; I needed both my hands to climb with and catch my horse, so for lack of a better place I took off my hat and said, "Bunny, how would you like to ride in that?" He wobbled his nose, which I understood to mean that he didn't care. So I put the Rabbit on my head, and put the hat on again.

Then I went forward and found that the cook had recovered his pots and pans; all was well now and my horse was awaiting me.

I rode all the rest of that day with the Rabbit quietly nestling in my hair. It was a long, hard day, for we continued till nightfall and then made a dark camp in a thick pine woods. It was impossible to make pictures then, so I put the little Rabbit under a leatheroid telescope lid, on a hard level place, gave him food and water, and left him for use in the morning.

THE RABBIT DANCE

About nine o'clock that night we were sitting about the fire, when from the near woods was heard a tremendous "tap-tap-taptrrr," so loud and so near that we all jumped and stared into the darkness. Again it came, "tap-tap-tap trrrrr," a regular drum tattoo.

"What is that?" we all exclaimed, and at that moment a large Rabbit darted across the open space lighted by the fire.

Again the tattoo and another Rabbit dashed across. Then it dawned on me that that was the young Rabbit signalling to his friends. He was using the side of his box for a drum.

Again the little prisoner rolled his signal call, and then a third Snowshoe Rabbit appeared.

"Look at all the Rabbits!" exclaimed my friend. "Where is my gun?"

"No," I said, "you don't need your gun. Wait and see. There is something up. That little chap is ringing up central."

"I never saw so many together in all my life," said he. Then added: "I've got an acetylene lantern; perhaps we can get a picture."

As soon as he had his camera and lantern, we went cautiously to the rabbity side of the woods; several ran past us. Then we sat down on a smooth place. My friend held the camera, I held the light, but we rested both on the ground. Very soon a Rabbit darted from the darkness into the great cone of light from the lantern, gazed at that wonder for a moment, gave a "thump" and disappeared. Then another came; then two or three. They gazed into this unspeakably dazzling thing, then one gave the alarm by thumping, and all were lost to sight.

But they came again and in ever-increasing numbers, 4, 5, 7, 8, 10 at last, now in plain view, gazing wildly at the bright light, pushing forward as though fascinated. Some two or three so close together that they were touching each other. Then one gave the thumping alarm, and all scattered like leaves, to vanish like ghosts. But they came back again, to push and crawl up nearer to that blazing wonder. Some of the back ones were skipping about but the front ones edged up in a sort of wild-eyed fascination. Closer and closer they got, then the first one was so near that reaching out to smell the lantern he burnt his nose, and at his alarm thump, all disappeared in the woods. But they soon returned to disport again in that amazing brightness; and, stimulated by the light, they danced about, chasing each other, dodging around in large circles till one of the outermost leaped over the camera box and another following him, leaped up and sat on it. My friend was just behind, hidden by the light in front, and he had no trouble in clutching the impudent Rabbit with both hands. Instantly it set up a loud squealing. The other Rabbits gave a stamping signal, and in a moment all were lost in the woods, but the one we held. Quickly we transported it to another leatheroid box, intending to take its picture in the morning, but the prisoner had a means of attack that I had not counted on. Just as we were going to sleep he began with his front feet on the resounding box and beat a veritable drum tattoo of alarm. Every one in camp was awakened, and again, as we were dropping off, the camp was roused by another loud "tattoo." For nearly two hours this went on; then, about midnight, utterly unable to sleep, I arose and let the drummer go about his business, do anything or go anywhere, so only he would be quiet and let us attend to ours.

Next morning I photographed the little Bunny, and set him free to join his kin. It is a surprising fact that though we spent two weeks in this valley, and a month in those mountains, we did not see another wild Rabbit.

This incident is unique in my experience. It is the only time when I found the Snowshoe Hares gathered for a social purpose, and is the only approach to a game that I ever heard of among them.

THE GHOST RABBIT

An entirely different side of Rabbit life is seen in another mysterious incident that I have never been able to explain.

At one time when I lived in Ontario, I had a very good hound that was trained to follow all kinds of trails. I used to take him out in the woods at night, give him general instructions "to go ahead, and report everything afoot"; then sit down on a log to listen to his reports. And he made them with remarkable promptness. Slight differences in his bark, and the course taken, enabled me to tell at once whether it was Fox, Coon, Rabbit, Skunk, or other local game. And his peculiar falsetto yelp when the creature treed, was a joyful invitation to "come and see for yourself."

The hound's bark for a Fox was deep, strong, and at regular intervals as befitted the strong trail, and the straightaway run. But for a Rabbit it was broken, uncertain, irregular and rarely a good deep bay.

One night the dog bawled in his usual way, "Rabbit, Rabbit, Rabbit," and soon leaving the woods he crossed an open field where the moon shone brightly, and I could easily see to follow. Still yelping "Rabbit, Rabbit, Rabbit," he dashed into a bramble thicket in the middle of the field. But at once he dashed out again shrieking, "Police! Help! Murder!" and took refuge behind me, cowering up against my legs. At the same moment from the side of that bramble thicket there went out--a Rabbit. Yes, a common Rabbit all right, but it was a snow-white one. The first albino Cottontail I had ever seen, and apparently the first albino Cottontail that[C] Ranger had ever seen. Dogs are not supposed to be superstitious, but on that occasion Ranger behaved exactly as though he thought that he had seen a ghost.

A NARROW-GAUGE MULE--THE PRAIRIE HARE

One has to see this creature with its great flopping ears, and its stiff-legged jumping like a bucking mule, to realize the aptness of its Western nickname.

As it bounds away from your pathway its bushy snow-white tail and the white behind the black-tipped ears will point out plainly that it is neither the Texas Jackrabbit nor the Rocky Mountain Cottontail, but the White-tailed Jackrabbit, the finest of all our Hares.

I have met it in woods, mountains, and prairies, from California to Manitoba and found it the wildest of its race and almost impossible of approach; except in the great exceptional spot, the Yellowstone Park. Here in the August of 1912 I met with two, close to the Mammoth Hot Springs Hotel. At a distance of thirty feet they gave me good chances to take pictures, and though the light was very bad I made a couple of snaps. Fifteen years ago, when first I roamed in the Park, the Prairie Hare was exceedingly rare, but now, like so many of the wild folk, it has become quite common. Another evidence of the efficacy of protection.

This silvery-gray creature turns pure white in the winter, when the snow mantle of his range might otherwise make it too conspicuous.

THE BUMP OF MOSS THAT SQUEAKS

No matter how horrible a certain climate or surroundings may seem to us, they are sure to be the ideal of some wild creature, its very dream of bliss. I suppose that slide rock, away up in cold, bleak, windy country above the timber-line, is absolutely the unloveliest landscape and most repulsive home ground that a man could find in the mountains and yet it is the paradise, the perfect place of a wonderful little creature that is found on the high peaks of the Rockies from California to Alaska.

It is not especially abundant in the Yellowstone Park, but it was there that first I made its acquaintance, and Easterners will meet with it in the great Reserve more often than in all other parts of its range put together.

As one reaches the Golden Gate, near Mammoth Hot Springs, many little animals of the Ground-squirrel group are seen running about, and from the distance comes a peculiar cry, a short squeak uttered every ten or fifteen seconds. You stop, perhaps search with your eye the remote hillside, but you are looking too far afield. Glance toward the tumbled rock piles, look at every high point. There on top of one you note a little gray lump, like a bump of moss, the size of your fist, clinging to the point of the rock. Fix your glasses on it, and you will see plainly that the squeak is made by this tiny creature, like a quarter-grown Rabbit with short, round, white-rimmed ears and no visible tail. This is the curious little animal that cannot be happy anywhere but in the slide rock; this is the Calling Hare. "Little Chief Hare" is its Indian name, but it has many others of much currency, such as "Pika," and "Starved Rat," the latter because it is never fat. The driver calls it a "Coney," or "Rock Rabbit." In its colour, size, shape, and habits it differs from all other creatures in the region; it is impossible to mistake it. Though a distant kinsman of the Rabbits, it is unlike them in looks and ways. Thus it has, as noted, the very un-rabbit-like habit of squeaking from some high lookout. This is doubtless a call of alarm to let the rest of the company know that there is danger about, for the Coney is a gregarious creature; there may be a hundred of them in the rock-slide.

Some years ago, in Colorado, I sketched one of the Coneys by help of a field glass. He was putting all the force of his energetic little soul into the utterance of an alarm cry for the benefit of his people.

But the most interesting habit of this un-rabbity Rabbit is its way of preparing for winter.

When the grass, the mountain dandelions, and the peavines are at their best growth for making hay, the Coney, with his kind, goes warily from his stronghold in the rocks to the nearest stretch of herbage, and there cuts as much as he can carry of the richest growths; then laden with a bundle as big as himself, and very much longer, he makes for the rocks, and on some flat open place spreads the herbage out to be cured for his winter hay. Out in full blaze of the sun he leave it, and if some inconsiderate rock comes in between, to cast a shadow on his hay a-curing, he moves the one that is easiest to move; he never neglects his hay. When dry enough to be safe, he packs it away into his barn, the barn being a sheltered crevice in the rocks where the weather cannot harm it, and where it will continue good until the winter time, when otherwise there would be a sad pinch of famine in the Coney world. The trappers say that they can tell whether the winter will be hard or open by the amount of food stored up in the Coney barns.

Many a one of these I have examined in the mountains of British Columbia and Colorado, as well as in the Park. The quantity of hay in them varies from what might fill a peck measure to what would make a huge armful. Among the food plants used, I found many species of grass, thistle, meadow-rue, peavine, heath, and the leaves of several composite plants. I suspect that fuller observations will show that they use every herb not actually poisonous, that grows in the vicinity of their citadel. More than one of these wads of hay had in the middle of it a nest or hollow; not, I suspect, the home nest where the young are raised, but a sort of winter restaurant where they could go while the ground was covered with snow, and sitting in the midst of their provisions, eat to their heart's content.

It is not unlikely that in this we see the growth of the storage habit, beginning first with a warm nest of hay, which it was found could be utilized for food when none other was available. The fact that these barns are used year after year is shown by the abundance of pellets in several layers which were found in and about them.

THE WEATHERWISE CONEY

A very wise little people is this little people of the Rocks. Not only do they realize that in summer they must prepare for winter, but they know how to face a present crisis, however unexpected. To appreciate the following instance, we must remember that the central thought in the Coney's life is his "grub pile" for winter use, and next that he is a strictly daytime animal. I have often slept near a Coney settlement and never heard a sound or seen a sign of their being about after dark. Nevertheless, Merriam tells us that he and Vernon Bailey once carried their blankets up to a Coney colony above timber-line in the Salmon River Mountains of Idaho, intending to spend the night there and to study the Coneys whose piles of hay were visible in all directions on their rocks. As this was about the first of September, it was natural to expect fair weather and a complete curing of the hay in a week or so. But a fierce storm set in with the descending night. The rain changed to hail and then to snow, and much to the surprise of the naturalists, they heard the squeak of the Coneys all night long.

These animals love the sunshine, the warmth and the daylight, and dread cold and darkness as much as we do. It must have been a bitter experience when at the call of the older ones every little Coney had to tumble out of his warm bed in the chill black hours and face the driving sleet to save the winter's supplies. But tumble out they did, and overtime they worked, hard and well, for when the morning dawned the slide-rock and the whole world was covered deep in snow, but every haycock had been removed to a safer place under the rocks, and the wisdom of the Coney once more exemplified, with adequate energy to make it effective.

HIS SAFETY IS IN THE ROCKS

No one has ever yet found the home nest of the Calling Hare. It is so securely hidden under rocks, and in galleries below rocks, that all attempts to dig it out have thus far failed. I know of several men, not to mention Bears, Badgers, Wolverines, and Grizzlies, who have essayed to unearth the secret of the Coney's inner life. Following on the trail of a Coney that bleated derisively at me near Pagoda Peak, Col., I began at once to roll rocks aside in an effort to follow him home to his den. The farther I went the less satisfaction I found. The uncertain trail ramified more and more as I laboured. Once or twice from far below me I heard a mocking squeak that spurred me on, but that too, ceased. When about ten tons of rock had been removed I was baffled. There were half a dozen possible lines of continuation, and while I paused to wipe the "honest sweat" from my well-meaning brow, I heard behind me the "weak," "weak," of my friend as though giving his estimate of my resolution, and I descried him--I suppose the same--on a rock point like a moss-bump against the sky-line away to the left. Only, one end of the moss-bump moved a little each time a squeak was cast upon the air. I had not time to tear down the whole mountain, so I did as my betters, the Bears and Badgers have done before me, I gave it up. I had at least found out why the Coney avoids the pleasant prairie and the fertile banks, and I finished with a new and profounder understanding of the Scripture text which says in effect,

"As for the Coney, his safe refuge is in the rocks."

FOOTNOTES:

[Footnote C: It proved later to be an albino domestic Rabbit run wild.]

* * * * *

X

Ghosts of the Campfire

* * * * *

X

Ghosts of the Campfire

It is always worth while to cultivate the old guides. Young guides are often fresh and shallow, but the quiet old fellows, that have spent their lives in the mountains, must be good or they could not stay in the business; and they have seen so much and been so far that they are like rare old manuscript volumes, difficult to read, but unique and full of value. It is not easy to get them to talk, but there is a combination that often does it. First, show yourself worthy of their respect by holding up your end, be it in an all-day climb or breakneck ride; then at night, after the others have gone to bed, you sit while the old guide smokes, and by a few brief questions and full attention, show that you value any observations he may choose to make. Many happy hours and much important information have been my reward for just such cautious play, and often as we sat, there flitted past, in the dim light, the silent shadowy forms of the campfire ghosts. Swift, not twinkling, but looming light and fading, absolutely silent. Sometimes approaching so near that the still watcher can get the glint of beady eyes or even of a snowy breast, for these ghosts are merely the common Mice of the mountains, abounding in every part of the West.

There are half a dozen different kinds, yet most travellers will be inclined to bunch them all, and pass them by as mere Mice. But they are worthy of better treatment. Three, at least, are so different in form and ways that you should remember them by their names.

First is the Whitefooted or Deer-mouse. This is the one that you find in the coffee pot or the water bucket in the morning; this is the one that skips out of the "grub box" when the cook begins breakfast; and this is the one that runs over your face with its cold feet as you sleep nights. It is one of the most widely diffused mammals in North America to-day, and probably the most numerous.

It is an elegant little creature, with large, lustrous black eyes like those of a Deer, a fact which, combined with its large ears, the fawn-coloured back, and the pure white breast, has given it the name of "Deer-mouse." It is noted for drumming with one foot as a call to its mate, and for uttering a succession of squeaks and trills that serve it as a song.

Sometimes its nest is underground; and sometimes in a tree, whence the name Tree-mouse. It breeds several times in a year and does not hibernate, so is compelled to lay up stores of food for winter use. To help it in doing this it has a very convenient pair of capacious pockets, one in each cheek, opening into the mouth.

THE JUMPING MOUSE

He glides around the fire much as the others do, but at the approach of danger, he simply fires himself out of a catapult, afar into the night. Eight or ten feet he can cover in one of these bounds and he can, and does, repeat them as often as necessary. How he avoids knocking out his own brains in his travels I have not been able to understand.

This is the New World counterpart of the Jerboa, so familiar in our school books as a sort of diminutive but glorified kangaroo that frequents the great Pyramids. It is so like a Jerboa in build and behaviour that I was greatly surprised and gratified to find my scientist friends quite willing that I should style it the American representative of the African group.

The country folk in the East will tell you that there are "seven sleepers" in our woods, and enumerate them thus: the Bear, the Coon, the Skunk, the

Woodchuck, the Chipmunk, the Bat, and the Jumping Mouse. All are good examples, but the longest, soundest sleeper of the whole somnolent brotherhood is the Jumping Mouse. Weeks before summer is ended it has prepared a warm nest deep underground, beyond the reach of cold or rain, and before the early frost has nipped the aster, the Jumping Mouse and his wife curl up with their long tails around themselves like cords on a spool, and sleep the deadest kind of a dead sleep, unbroken by even a snore, until summer is again in the land, and frost and snow unknown. This means at least seven months on the Yellowstone.

Since the creature is chiefly nocturnal, the traveller is not likely to see it, excepting late at night when venturesome individuals often come creeping about the campfire, looking for scraps or crumbs; or sometimes other reckless youngsters of the race, going forth to seek their fortunes, are found drowned in the tanks or wells about the hotels.

Here is a diagram of a Jumper in the act of living up to its reputation. And at once one asks what is the reason for this interminable tail. The answer is, it is the tail to the kite, the feathering to the arrow; and observation shows that a Jumping Mouse that has lost its tail is almost helpless to escape from danger. A good naturalist records that one individual that was de-tailed by a mowing machine, jumped frantically and far, but had no control of the direction, and just as often as not went straight up or landed wrong end to, and sometimes on a second bound was back where it had started from.

It is very safe to say that all unusual developments serve a very vital purpose in the life of the creature, but we are not always so fortunate as in this case, to know what that purpose is.

THE CALLING MOUSE

One day fifteen years ago I was sitting on a low bank near Baronett's Bridge across the Yellowstone, a mile and a half from Yancey's. The bank was in an open place, remote from cliffs or thick woods; it was high, dry, and dotted with holes of rather larger than field-mouse size, which were further peculiar in that most of them went straight down and none was connected with any visible overland runways.

All of which is secondary to the fact that I was led to the bank by a peculiar bleating noise like the "weak" of a Calling Hare, but higher pitched.

As I passed the place the squeakers were left behind me, and so at last I traced the noise to some creature underground. But what it was I could not see or determine. I knew only from the size of the hole it must be as small as a Mouse.

Not far away from this I drew some tracks I found in the dust, and later when I showed the drawing, and told the story to a naturalist friend, he said: "I had the same experience in that country once, and was puzzled until I found out by keeping a captive that the creature in the bank was a Grasshopper Mouse or a Calling Mouse, and those in your drawing are its tracks."

At one time it was considered an extremely rare animal, but now, having discovered its range, we know it to be quite abundant. In northern New Mexico I found one species so common in the corn-field that I could catch two or three every night with a few mousetraps. But it is scarce on the Yellowstone, and all my attempts to trap it were frustrated by the much more abundant Deer-mice, which sprang the bait and sacrificed themselves, every time I tried for the Squeaker.

In the fall of 1912 I was staying at Standing Rock Agency in North Dakota. On the broken ground, between the river and the high level prairie, I noted a ridge with holes exactly like those I had seen on the Yellowstone. A faint squeak underground gave additional and corroborative evidence. So I set a trap and next night had a specimen of the Squeaker as well as a couple of the omnipresent Deer-mice.

Doubtless the Calling Mouse has an interesting and peculiar life history, but little is known of it except that it dwells on the dry plains, is a caller by habit;-- through not around the campfire--it feeds largely on grasshoppers, and is in mortal terror of ants.

* * * * *

XI

Sneak-cats Big and Small

* * * * *

Sneak-cats--Big and Small

You may ride five hundred miles among the mountains, in a country where these beasts of prey abound, and yet see never a hair of a living Wildcat. But how many do you suppose see you? Peeping from a thicket, near the trail, glimpsing you across some open valley in the mountains, or inspecting you from various points as you recline by the campfire, they size you up and decide they want no nearer dealings with you; you are bad medicine, a thing to be eluded. And oh! how clever they are at eluding us.

If you turn out the biggest Lynx on the smoothest prairie you ever saw, he will efface himself before you count twenty. The grass may be but three inches high and the Lynx twenty-three, but he will melt into it, and wholly escape the searching eyes of the keenest. One would not think an empty skin could lie more flat. Add to this the silent sinuosity of his glide; he seems to ooze around the bumps and stumps, and bottle up his frightful energy for the final fearsome leap. His whole makeup is sacrificed to efficiency in that leap; on that depends his life; his very existence turns on the wondrous perfection of the sneak, of which the leap is the culmination. Hunters in all parts where these creatures abound, agree in calling Wildcat, Lynx, and Cougar by the undignified but descriptive name of Sneak-cat.

THE BOBCAT OR MOUNTAIN WILDCAT

The Wildcat of Europe, and of literature, is a creature of almost unparalleled ferocity. Our own Wildcat is three times as big and heavy, so many persons assume that it is three times as ferocious, and therefore to be dreaded almost like a Tiger. The fact is, the American Wildcat or Bobcat is a very shy creature, ready to run from a very small dog, never facing a man and rarely killing anything bigger than a Rabbit.

I never saw but one Bobcat in the Yellowstone Park, and that was not in the Park, but at Gardiner where it was held a captive. But it came from the Park, and the guides tell me that the species is quite common in some localities.

It is readily recognized by its cat-like form and its short or bob-tail, whence its name.

MISUNDERSTOOD--THE CANADA LYNX

The southern part of North America is occupied by Bobcats of various kinds, the northern part by Lynxes, their very near kin, and there is a narrow belt of middle territory occupied by both. The Yellowstone Park happens to be in that belt, so we find here both the Mountain Bobcat and the Canada Lynx.

I remember well three scenes from my childhood days in Canada, in which this animal was the central figure. A timid neighbour of ours was surprised one day to see a large Lynx come out of the woods in broad daylight, and walk toward his house. He went inside, got his gun, opened the door a little, and knelt down. The Lynx walked around the house at about forty yards distance, the man covering it with the gun most of the time, but his hand was shaking, the gun was wabbling, and he was tormented with the thought, "What if I miss, then that brute will come right at me, and then, oh, dear! what?"

He had not the nerve to fire and the Lynx walked back to the woods. How well I remember that man. A kind-hearted, good fellow, but oh! so timid. His neighbours guyed him about it, until at last he sold out his farm and joined the ministry.

The next scene was similar. Two men were out Coon-hunting, when their dogs treed something. A blazing fire soon made, showed plainly aloft in the tree the whiskered head of a Lynx. The younger man levelled his gun at it, but the other clung to his arm begging him to come away, reminding him that both had families dependent on them, and earnestly protesting that the Lynx, if wounded, would certainly come down and kill the whole outfit.

The third was wholly different. In broad daylight a Lynx came out of the woods near a settler's house, entered the pasture and seized a lamb. The good wife heard the noise of the sheep rushing, and went out in time to see the Lynx dragging the victim. She seized a stick and went for the robber. He growled defiantly, but at the first blow of the stick he dropped the lamb and ran. Then that plucky woman carried the lamb to the house; finding four deep cuts in its neck she sewed them up, and after a few days of careful nursing restored the woolly one to its mother, fully recovered.

The first two incidents illustrate the crazy ideas that some folks have about the Lynx, and the last shows what the real character of the animal is.

I have once or twice been followed by Lynxes, but I am sure it was merely out of curiosity. Many times I have met them in the woods at close range and each time they have gazed at me in a sort of mild-eyed wonder. There was no trace of ferocity in the gaze, but rather of innocent confidence.

The earliest meeting I ever had with a Lynx I shall remember when all the other meetings have been dimmed by time, but I have used the incident without embellishment in the early part of "Two Little Savages," so shall not repeat it here.

THE SHYEST THING IN THE WOODS--MOUNTAIN LION, PUMA OR COUGAR

Reference to the official report shows that there are about one hundred Mountain Lions now ranging the Yellowstone Park. And yet one is very safe in believing that not twenty-five persons of those living in the Park have ever seen one.

By way of contrast, the report gives the number of Blackbear at the same-- about one hundred--and yet every one living in the Park or passing through, has seen scores of Bears.

Why this difference? Chiefly owing to their respective habits. The Cougar is the most elusive, sneaking, adroit hider, and shyest thing in the woods. I have camped for twenty-five years in its country and have never yet seen a wild Cougar. Almost never are they found without dogs specially trained to trail and hunt them.

Although I have never seen a Cougar at large, it is quite certain that many a one has watched me. Yes! even in the Yellowstone Park. Remember this, oh traveller, sitting in front of the Mammoth Hot Springs Hotel! you are in sight of two famous Cougar haunts--Mt. Evarts and Bunsen Peak, and the chances are that, as you sit and perhaps read these lines, a Cougar lolling gray-brown among the gray-brown rocks of the mountain opposite, is calmly surveying all the world about, including yourself.

If you consult the witching contraband books that we of a bygone age used to read surreptitiously in school hours, you will learn that "the Cougar is a fearsome beast of invincible prowess. He can kill a Buffalo or an ox with a blow of his paw, and run off with it at full speed or carry it up a tree to devour, and he is by choice a man-eater. Commonly uttering the cry of a woman in distress to decoy the gallant victim to his doom." If, on the other hand, you consult some careful natural histories, or one or two of the seasoned guides, you learn that the Cougar, though horribly destructive among Deer, sheep, and colts, rarely kills a larger prey, and never is known to attack man.

I have had many persons take exception to the last statement, and give contrary proof by referring to some hair-lifting incident which seemed to be a refutation. But most of these attacks by Cougars have failed to stand the disintegrating power of a carefully focussed searchlight.

There is no doubt that the Cougar is addicted to horseflesh, as his scientific name implies (hippolestes=horse pirate). He will go a long way to kill a colt, and several supposed cases of a Cougar attacking a man on horseback at night prove to have been attacks on the horse, and in each case on discovering the man the Cougar had decamped.

This creature is also possessed of a strong curiosity and many times is known to have followed a man in the woods merely to study the queer creature, but without intent to do him harm. Nevertheless the timid traveller who discovers he is "pursued by a Cougar" may manage to persuade himself that he has had a hairbreadth escape.

THE TIME I MET A LION

A newspaper reporter asked me once for a story of terrible peril from our wild animals, a time "when I nearly lost my life."

My answer was, "I never had such an experience. Danger from wild animals is practically non-existent in America to-day."

"Did you never meet a Grizzly or a Mountain Lion?" he asked.

"Yes, many Grizzlies, and one or two Lions. I've had one look me over while I slept," was the answer.

And now the thrill-monger's face lighted up, he straightened his paper and stuck his pencil in his mouth by way of getting ready, and ejaculated: "Say! now you're getting it; let's hear the details. Don't spare me!"

"It was back in September, 1899," I said. "My wife and I were camping in the high Sierra near Mt. Tallac. At this season rain is unknown, so we took no tent. Each of us had a comfortable rubber bed and we placed these about a foot or two apart. In the narrow alley between we put a waterproof canvas, and on that each night we laid the guns.

"We had a couple of cowboys to look after the outfit. A fortnight had gone by with sunny skies and calm autumn weather, when one evening it began to blow. Black, lumpy clouds came up from the far-off sea; the dust went whirling in little eddies, and when the sun went down it was of a sickly yellowish. The horses were uneasy, throwing up their noses, snorting softly and pricking their ears in a nervous way.

"Everything promised a storm in spite of the rule 'no rain in September,' and we huddled into our tentless beds with such preparation as we could make for rain.

"As night wore on the windstorm raged, and one or two heavy drops spattered down. Then there was a loud snort or two and a plunge of the nearest horse, then quiet.

"Next morning we found every horse gone, and halters and ropes broken, while deep hoofprints showed the violence of the stampede which we had scarcely heard. The men set out on foot after the horses, and by good luck, recovered all within a mile. Meanwhile I made a careful study of the ground, and soon got light. For there were the prints of a huge Mountain Lion. He had prowled into camp, coming up to where we slept, sneaked around and smelt us over, and--I think--walked down the alley between our beds. After that, probably, he had got so close to the horses that, inspired by terror of their most dreaded foe, they had broken all bonds and stampeded into safety. Nevertheless, though the horses were in danger, there can be no question, I think, that we were not."

The reporter thought the situation more serious than I did, and persisted that if I dug in my memory I should yet recall a really perilous predicament, in which thanks to some wild brute, I was near death's door. And as it proved he was right. I had nearly forgotten what looked like a hairbreadth escape.

IN PERIL OF MY LIFE

It was on the same Sierra trip. Our outfit had been living for weeks among the tall pines, subsisting on canned goods; and when at length we came out on the meadows by Leaf Lake we found them enlivened by a small herd of wild--that is, range-cattle.

"My!" said one of the cowboys, "wouldn't a little fresh milk go fine after all that ptomaine we've been feeding on?"

"There's plenty of it there; help yourself," said I.

"I'd soon catch one if I knew which, and what to do when I got her," he answered.

Then memories of boyhood days on the farm came over me and I said: "I'll show you a cow in milk, and I'll milk her if you'll hold her."

"Agreed! Which is the one?"

I put my hands up to my mouth and let off a long bleat like a calf in distress. The distant cattle threw up their heads and began "sniffing." Another bleat and three cows separated from the others; two ran like mad into the woods, the third kept throwing her head this way and that, but not running. "That one," I said, "is your cow. She's in milk and not too recently come in."

Then away went the cowboys to do their part. The herd scattered and the cow tried to run, but the ponies sailed alongside, the lariats whistled and in a flash she was held with one rope around her horns, the other around one hind leg.

"Now's your chance, Milk-lady!" they shouted at me, and forward I went, pail in hand, to milk that snorting, straining, wild-eyed thing. She tried to hold her milk up, but I am an old hand at that work. She never ceased trying to kick at me with her free hind leg, so I had to watch the leg, and milk away. The high pitched "tsee tsee" had gradually given place to the low "tsow tsow" of the two streams cutting the foam when a peculiar smell grew stronger until it was nothing less than a disgusting stench. For the first time I glanced down at the milk in the pail, and there instead of a dimpled bank of snowy foam was a great yeasty mass of yellowish brown streaked with blood.

Hastily rising and backing off, I said: "I've got plenty of milk now for you two. The rest of us don't care for any. Hold on till I get back to the trees."

Then, when I was safely under cover, the boys turned the cow loose. Of course, her first impulse was revenge, but I was safe and those mounted men knew how to handle a cow. She was glad to run off.

"There's your milk," I said, and pointed to the pail I had left. Evidently that cow had been suffering from more than one milk malady. The boys upset the bloody milk right there, then took the pail to the stream, where they washed it well, and back to camp, where we scalded it out several times.

THE DANGEROUS NIGHT VISITOR

That night about sundown, just as we finished supper, there came from the near prairie the mighty, portentous rumbling roar of a bull--the bellow that he utters when he is roused to fight, the savage roar that means "I smell blood." It is one of those tremendous menacing sounds that never fail to give one the creeps and make one feel, oh! so puny and helpless.

We went quietly to the edge of the timber and there was the monster at the place where that evil milk was spilt, tearing up the ground with hoofs and horns, and uttering that dreadful war-bellow. The cowboys mounted their ponies, and gave a good demonstration of the power of brains in the ruling of brawn. They took that bull at a gallop a mile or more away, they admonished him with some hard licks of a knotted-rope and left him, then came back, and after a while we all turned in for the night.

Just as we were forgetting all things, the sweet silence of the camp was again disturbed by that deep, vibrating organ tone, the chesty roaring of the enraged bull; and we sprang up to see the huge brute striding in the moonlight, coming right into camp, lured as before by that sinister blood trail.

The boys arose and again saddled the ready mounts. Again I heard the thudding of heavy feet, the shouts of the riders, a few loud snorts, followed by the silence; and when the boys came back in half an hour we rolled up once more and speedily were asleep.

To pass the night in peace! not at all. Near midnight my dreams were mixed with earthquakes and thunder, and slowly I waked to feel that ponderous bellow running along the ground, and setting my legs a-quiver.

"Row-ow-ow-ow" it came, and shook me into full wakefulness to realize that that awful brute was back again. He could not resist the glorious, alluring chance to come and get awfully mad over that "bluggy milk." Now he was in camp, close at hand; the whole sky seemed blocked out and the trees a-shiver as he came on.

"Row-ow-ow-ow" he rumbled, also snorted softly as he came, and before I knew it he walked down the narrow space between our beds and the wagon. Had I jumped up and yelled, he, whether mad or scared, might have trampled one or other of us. That is the bull of it; a horse steps over. So I waited in trembling silence till that horrid "Row-ow-ow-ow" went by. Then I arose and yelled with all my power:

"Louie! Frank! Help! Here's the bull."

The boys were up before I had finished. The ready ponies were put in commission in less than three minutes. Then came the stampede, the heavy thudding, the loud whacks of the ropes, and when these sounds had died in the distance, I heard the "pop, pop" of side arms. I asked no questions, but when the boys came back and said, "well, you bet he won't be here again," I believed them.

* * * * *

XII

Bears of High and Low Degree

* * * * *

XII

Bears of High and Low Degree

Why is snoring a crime at night and a joke by day? It seems to be so, and the common sense of the public mind so views it.

In the September of 1912 I went with a good guide and a party of friends, to the region southeast of Yellowstone Lake. This is quite the wildest part of the Park; it is the farthest possible from human dwellings, and in it the animals are wild and quite unchanged by daily association with man, as pensioners of the hotels.

Our party was carefully selected, a lot of choice spirits, and yet there was one with a sad and unpardonable weakness--he always snored a dreadful snore as soon as he fell asleep. That is why he was usually put in a tent by himself, and sent to sleep with a twenty-five foot deadening space between him and us of gentler somnolence.

He had been bad the night before, and now, by request, was sleeping fifty feet away. But what is fifty feet of midnight silence to a forty-inch chest and a pair of tuneful nostrils. About 2 A.M. I was awakened as before, but worse than ever, by the most terrific, measured snorts, and so loud that they seemed just next me. Sitting up, I bawled in wrath, "Oh, Jack, shut up, and let some one else have a chance to sleep."

The answer was a louder snort, a crashing of brush and a silence that, so far as I know, continued until sunrise.

Then I arose and learned that the snorts and the racket were made, not by my friend, but by a huge Grizzly that had come prowling about the camp, and had awakened me by snorting into my tent.

But he had fled in fear at my yell; and this behaviour exactly shows the attitude of the Grizzlies in the West to-day. They are afraid of man, they fly at whiff or sound of him, and if in the Yellowstone you run across a Grizzly that seems aggressive, rest assured he has been taught such bad manners by association with our own species around the hotels.

THE DIFFERENT KINDS OF BEARS

Some guides of unsound information will tell the traveller that there are half a dozen different kinds of Bears in or near the Yellowstone Park--Blackbear, Little Cinnamon, Big Cinnamon, Grizzlies, Silver-tip, and Roach-backs. This is sure however, there are but two species, namely, the Blackbear and the Grizzly.

The Blackbear is known by its short front claws, flat profile and black colour, with or without a tan-coloured muzzle. Sometimes in a family of Blackbears there appears a red-headed youngster, just as with ourselves; he is much like his brethren but "all over red complected" as they say in Canada. This is known to hunters as a "Little Cinnamon."

The Grizzly is known by its great size, its long fore claws, its hollow profile and its silver-sprinkled coat. Sometimes a Grizzly has an excessive amount of silver; this makes a Silver-tip. Sometimes the silver is nearly absent, in which case the Bear is called a "Big Cinnamon." Sometimes the short mane over his humped shoulders is exaggerated; this makes a "Roach-back." Any or all of these are to be looked for in the Park, yet remember! they form only two species. All of the Blackbear group are good climbers; none of the Grizzly group climb after they are fully grown.

BEAR-TREES

There is a curious habit of Bears that is well known without being well understood; it is common to all these mentioned. In travelling along some familiar trail they will stop at a certain tree, claw it, tear it with their teeth, and rub their back and head up against it as high as they can reach, even with the tip of the snout, and standing on tiptoes. There can be no doubt that a Bear coming to a tree can tell by scent whether another Bear has been there recently, and whether that Bear is a male or female, a friend, a foe or a stranger. Thus the tree serves as a sort of news depot; and there is one every few hundred yards in country with a large Bear population.

These trees, of course, abound in the Park. Any good guide will point out some examples. In the country south of the Lake, I found them so common that it seemed as if the Bears had made many of them for mere sport.

A PEEP INTO BEAR FAMILY LIFE

When we went to the Yellowstone in 1897 to spend the season studying wild animal life, we lived in a small shanty that stood near Yancey's, and had many pleasant meetings with Antelope, Beaver, etc., but were disappointed in not seeing any Bears. One of my reasons for coming was the promise of "as many Bears as I liked." But some tracks on the trail a mile away were the only proofs that I found of Bears being in the region.

One day General Young, then in charge of the Park, came to see how we were getting along. And I told him that although I had been promised as many Bears as I liked, and I had been there investigating for six weeks already, I hadn't seen any. He replied, "You are not in the right place. Go over to the Fountain Hotel and there you will see as many Bears as you wish." That was impossible, for there were not Bears enough in the West to satisfy me, I thought. But I went at once to the Fountain Hotel and without loss of time stepped out the back door.

I had not gone fifty feet before I walked onto a big Blackbear with her two roly-poly black cubs. The latter were having a boxing match, while the mother sat by to see fair play. As soon as they saw me they stopped their boxing, and as soon as I saw them I stopped walking. The old Bear gave a peculiar "Koff koff," I suppose of warning, for the young ones ran to a tree, and up that they shinned with alacrity that amazed me. When safely aloft, they sat like small boys, holding on with their hands, while their little black legs dangled in the air, and waited to see what was to happen down below.

The mother Bear, still on her hind legs, came slowly toward me, and I began to feel very uncomfortable indeed, for she stood about six feet high in her stocking feet, and I had not even a stick to defend myself with. I began backing slowly toward the hotel, and by way of my best defense, I turned on her all the power of my magnetic eye. We have all of us heard of the wonderful power of the magnetic human eye. Yes, we have, but apparently this old Bear had not, for she came on just the same. She gave a low woof, and I was about to abandon all attempts at dignity, and run for the hotel; but just at this turning-point the old Bear stopped, and gazed at me calmly.

Then she faced about and waddled over to the tree, up which were the cubs. Underneath she stood, looking first at me, then at her family. I realized that she wasn't going to bother me, in fact she never seemed very serious about it, so I plucked up courage. I remembered what I came for and got down my camera. But when I glanced at the sky, and gauged the light--near sundown in the woods--I knew the camera would not serve me; so I got out my sketch book instead, and made the sketch which is given on Plate XXXVIII; I have not changed it since.

Meanwhile the old Bear had been sizing me up, and evidently made up her mind that, "although that human being might be all right, she would take no chances for her little ones."

She looked up to her two hopefuls, and gave a peculiar whining "Er-r-r er-r," whereupon, like obedient children, they jumped as at the word of command. There was nothing about them heavy or bear-like as commonly understood; lightly they swung from bough to bough till they dropped to the ground, and all went off together into the woods.

I was much tickled by the prompt obedience of these little Bears. As soon as their mother told them to do something they did it. They did not even offer a suggestion. But I also found out that there was a good reason back of it, for, had they not done as she had told them, they would have got such a spanking as would have made them howl. Yes, it is quite the usual thing, I find, for an old Blackbear to spank her little ones when in her opinion they need it, and she lays it on well. She has a good strong paw, and does not stop for their squealing; so that one correction lasts a long time.

This was a delightful peep into Bear home-life, and would have been well worth coming for, if the insight had ended there. But my friends in the hotel said that that was not the best place for Bears. I should go to the garbage-heap, a quarter-mile off in the forest. There, they said, I surely could see as many Bears as I wished, which was absurd of them.

THE DAY AT THE GARBAGE PILE

Early next morning I equipped myself with pencils, paper and a camera, and set out for the garbage pile. At first I watched from the bushes, some seventy-five yards away, but later I made a hole in the odorous pile itself, and stayed there all day long, sketching and snapshotting the Bears which came and went in greater numbers as the day was closing.

A sample of my notes made on the spot will illustrate the continuity of the Bear procession, yet I am told that there are far more of these animals there to-day than at the time of my visit.

Those readers who would follow my adventures in detail will find them fully and exactly set forth in the story of Johnny Bear, which appears in "Lives of the Hunted," so I shall not further enlarge on them here, except to relate one part which was omitted, as it dealt with a photographic experience.

In the story I told how, backed by a mounted cowboy, I sat on the garbage pile while the great Grizzly that had worsted Old Grumpy, came striding nearer, and looming larger.

He had not quite forgotten the recent battle, his whole air was menacing, and I had all the appropriate sensations as he approached. At forty yards I snapped him, and again at twenty. Still he was coming, but at fifteen feet he stopped and turned his head, giving me the side view I wanted, and I snapped the camera again. The effect was startling. That insolent, nagging little click brought the wrath of the Grizzly onto myself. He turned on me with a savage growl. I was feeling just as I should be feeling; wondering, indeed, if my last moment had not come, but I found guidance in the old adage: "when you don't know a thing to do, don't do a thing." For a minute or two the Grizzly glared, and I remained still; then calmly ignoring me he set about his feast.

All of this I tell in detail in my story. But there was one thing I did not dare to do then; that was show the snaps I made.

Surely it would be a wonderful evidence of my courage and coolness if I could show a photograph of that big Grizzly when he was coming on--maybe to kill me--I did not know, but I had a dim vision of my sorrowing relatives developing the plate to see how it happened, for I pressed the button at the right time. The picture, such as it is, I give as Plate XL, c. I was so calm and cool and collected that I quite forgot to focus the camera.

LONESOME JOHNNY

During all this time Johnny had been bemoaning his sad lot, at the top of the tree; there I left him, still lamenting. That was the last I ever saw of him. In my story of Johnny Bear, I relate many other adventures that were ascribed to him, but these were told me by the men who lived in the Park, and knew the lame cub much better than I did. My own acquaintance with him was all within the compass of the one day I spent in the garbage-pile.

It is worthy of note that although Johnny died that autumn, they have had him every year ever since; and some years they have had two for the satisfaction of visitors who have read up properly before coming to the Park. Indeed, when I went back to the Fountain Hotel fifteen years afterward, a little Bear came and whined under my window about dawn, and the hotel folk assured me it was Little Johnny calling on his creator.

FURTHER ANNALS OF THE SANCTUARY

All of this was fifteen years ago. Since then there have been some interesting changes, but they are in the line of growth. Thirteen Bears in view at one time was my highest record, and that after sundown; but I am told that as many as twenty or twenty-five Bears are now to be seen there at once in June and July, when the wildwood foods are scarce. Most of them are Blackbears, but there are always a few Grizzlies about.

In view of their reputation, their numbers and the gradual removal of the restraining fear of men, one wonders whether these creatures are not a serious menace to the human dwellers of the Park. The fundamental peacefulness of the unhungry animal world is wonderfully brought out by the groups of huge shaggy monsters about the hotels.

At one time, and for long it was said, and truthfully, that the Bears in the Park had never abused the confidence man had placed in them. But one or two encounters have taken place to prove the exception.

An enthusiastic camera-hunter, after hearing of my experiences at the garbage pile, went there some years later, duly equipped to profit by the opportunity.

A large she Bear, with a couple of cubs appeared, but they hovered at a distance and did not give the artist a fair chance. He waited a long time, then seeing that they would not come to him, he decided to go to them. Quitting that sheltering hole, he sneaked along; crouching low and holding the camera ready, he rapidly approached the family group. When the young ones saw this strange two-legged beast coming threateningly near them, they took alarm and ran whining to their mother. All her maternal wrath was aroused to see this smallish, two-legged, one-eyed creature, evidently chasing her cubs to harm them. A less combination than that would have made her take the war-path, and now she charged. She struck him but once; that was enough. His camera was wrecked, and for two weeks afterward he was in the hospital, nursing three broken ribs, as well as a body suffering from shock.

There was another, an old Grizzly that became a nuisance about the hotels, as he did not hesitate to walk into the kitchens and help himself to food. Around the tents of campers he became a terror, as he soon realized that these folk carried food, and white canvas walls rising in the woods were merely invitations to a dinner ready and waiting. It is not recorded that he hurt any one in his numerous raids for food. But he stampeded horses and broke the camp equipments, as well as pillaged many larders.

One of my guides described a lively scene in which the Bear, in spite of blazing brands, ran into the cook's quarters and secured a ham. The cook pursued with a stick of firewood. At each whack the Bear let off a "whoof" but he did not drop the ham, and the party had to return to Fort Yellowstone for supplies.

Incidents of this kind multiplied, and finally Buffalo Jones, who was then the Chief Scout of the Park, was permitted to punish the old sinner. Mounted on his trained saddle-horse, swinging the lasso that has caught so many different kinds of beasts in so many different lands, the Colonel gave chase. Old Grizzly dodged among the pines for a while, but the pony was good to follow; and when the culprit took to open ground, the unerring lasso whistled in the air and seized him by the hind paw. It takes a good rope to stand the jerk of half a ton of savage muscle, but the rope was strong; it stood, and there was some pretty manoeuvring, after which the lasso was found over a high branch, with a couple of horses on the "Jones end" and they hauled the Bear aloft where, through the medium of a stout club, he received a drubbing that has become famous in the moving-picture world.

Another of these big, spoiled babies was sent to Washington Zoo, where he is now doing duty as an exhibition Grizzly.

The comedy element is far from lacking in this life; in fact, it is probably the dominant one. But the most grotesque story of all was told me by a friend who chummed with the Bears about ten years ago.

One day, it seems, a Blackbear more tame than usual went right into the bar-room of one of the hotels. The timid floating population moved out; the bar-keep was cornered, but somewhat protected by his bar; and when the Bear reared up with both paws on the mahogany, the wily "dispenser" pushed a glass of beer across, saying nervously, "Is that what you are after?"

The Bear liked the smell of the offering, and, stooping down, lapped up the whole glassful, and what was spilt he carefully licked up afterward, to the unmeasured joy of the loafers who peeped in at doors and windows, and jeered at the bar-keep and his new customer.

"Say, bar-keep, who's to pay?" "Don't you draw any color line?" "If I come in a fur coat, will you treat me?" "No! you got to scare him to drink free," etc., etc., were examples of their remarks.

Whatever that Bear came for, she seemed satisfied with what she got, for she went off peaceably to the woods, and was seen later lying asleep under a tree. Next day, however, she was back again. The scene in the bar-room was repeated with less intensity.

On the third and fourth days she came as before, but on the fifth day she seemed to want something else. Prompted by a kindred feeling, one of the loafers suggested that "She wants another round." His guess was right, and having got it, that abandoned old Bear began to reel, but she was quite good-natured about it, and at length lay down under a table, where her loud snores proclaimed to all that she was asleep--beastly drunk, and asleep--just like one of the lords of creation.

From that time on she became a habitual frequenter of the bar-room. Her potations were increased each month. There was a time when one glass of beer made her happy, but now it takes three or four, and sometimes even a little drop of something stronger. But whatever it is, it has the desired effect, and "Swizzling Jinnie" lurches over to the table, under which she sprawls at length, and tuning up her nasophone she sleeps aloud, and unpeacefully, demonstrating to all the world that after all a "Bear is jest a kind o' a man in a fur coat." Who can doubt it that reads this tale, for it is true; at least it was told me for the truth, by no less an authority than one of Jennie's intimate associates at the bar-room.

THE GRIZZLY AND THE CAN

When one remembers the Grizzly Bear as the monarch of the mountains, the king of the plains, and the one of matchless might and unquestioned sway among the wild things of the West, it gives one a shock to think of him being conquered and cowed by a little tin can. Yet he was, and this is how it came about.

A grand old Grizzly, that was among the summer retinue of a Park hotel, was working with two claws to get out the very last morsel of some exceptionally delicious canned stuff. The can was extra strong, its ragged edges were turned in, and presently both toes of the Bear were wedged firmly in the clutch of that impossible, horrid little tin trap. The monster shook his paw, and battered the enemy, but it was as sharp within as it was smooth without, and it gripped his paw with the fell clutch of a disease. His toes began to swell with all this effort and violence, till they filled the inner space completely. The trouble was made worse and the paw became painfully inflamed.

All day long that old Grizzly was heard clumping around with that dreadful little tin pot wedged on his foot. Sometimes there was a loud succession of clamp, clamp, clamp's which told that the enraged monarch with canned toes was venting his rage on some of the neighbouring Blackbears.

The next day and the next that shiny tin maintained its frightful grip on the Grizzly, who, limping noisily around, was known and recognized as "Can-foot." His comings and goings to and from the garbage heap, by day and by night, were plainly announced to all by the clamp, clamp, clamp of that maddening, galling tin. Some weeks went by and still the implacable meat box held on.

The officer in charge of the Park came riding by one day; he heard the strange tale of trouble, and saw with his own eyes the limping Grizzly, with his muzzled foot. At a wave of his hand two of the trusty scouts of the Park patrol set out with their ponies and whistling lassoes on the strangest errand that they, or any of their kind, had ever known. In a few minutes those wonderful raw-hide ropes had seized him and the monarch of the mountains was a prisoner bound. Strong shears were at hand. That vicious little can was ripped open. It was completely filled now with the swollen toes. The surgeon dressed the wounds, and the Grizzly was set free. His first blind animal impulse was to attack his seeming tormenters, but they were wise and the ponies were bear-broken; they easily avoided the charge, and he hastened to the woods to recover, finally, both his health and his good temper, and continue about the Park, the only full-grown Grizzly Bear, probably, that man ever captured to help in time of trouble, and then set loose again to live his life in peace.

* * * * *

Appendix

Mammals of the Yellowstone Park

* * * * *

Appendix

Mammals of the Yellowstone Park

A LIST OF THE SPECIES FOUND IN THE PARK IN 1912

BY ERNEST THOMPSON SETON

With assistance from the U. S. Biological Survey, and Colonel L. M. Brett, in charge of the Park.

Elk or Wapiti (Cervus canadensis) Abundant. By actual official count, and estimate of stray bands, they number at least 35,000, of which about 5,000 winter in the Park.

Mule Deer or Rocky Mt. Blacktail (Odocoileus heminus) Common. The official census gives their number at 400, of which at least 100 winter about Fort Yellowstone.

Whitetail Deer (Odocoileus virginianus macrourus) A few found about Gardiner, on Willow Creek, on Indian Creek, at Crevasse Mt. and in Cottonwood Basin. The official census gives their number at 100.

Moose (Alces americanus) Formerly rare, now abundant in all the southerly third of the Park. In 1897 they were estimated at 50. The official census gives their number at 550 in 1912.

Antelope or Pronghorn (Antilocapra americana) Formerly abundant, now rare; found only in broad open places such as Lamar Valley, etc. Their numbers have shrunk from many thousands in the '70's to about 1,500 in 1897, and 500 in 1912.

Mountain Sheep or Bighorn (Ovis canadensis) Formerly rare, now common about Mt. Evarts, Mt. Washburn and the western boundary. In 1897 there were about 100, perhaps only 75; in 1912 they are reported numbering 210 by actual count.

American Buffalo or Bison (Bison bison) Steadily increasing. In 1897 there were about 30; they now number 199 by actual count. These are in two herds, of 49 wild, and 150 in the fenced corrals.

Richardson Red-squirrel (Sciurus hudsonicus richardsoni) Abundant in all pine woods.

Northern Chipmunk (Eutamias quadrivittatus luteiventris) Extremely abundant everywhere.

Least Chipmunk (Eutamias minimus pictus) Common about Mammoth Hot Springs.

Golden Ground-squirrel (Citellus lateralis cinerascens) Common.

Picket-pin Ground-squirrel (Citellus armatus) Abundant on all level prairies.

Prairie-dog (Cynomys ludovicianus) Gen. Geo. S. Anderson told me long ago that the Prairie-dogs, so abundant on the Lower Yellowstone, were sometimes seen as far up as the Park at Gardiner.

[Illustration: XLVII. Johnnie Bear: his sins and his troubles Sketches by E. T. Seton]

[Illustration: XLVIII. Johnnie happy at last Photo by Miss L. Griscom]

Yellow Woodchuck, Rock Chuck or Marmot (Marmota flaviventer) Abundant on all mountains.

Rocky Mt. Flying Squirrel (Sciuropterus alpinus) Said to be found. I did not see one.

Beaver (Castor canadensis) Abundant and increasing.

Grasshopper Mouse (Onychomys leucogaster) I found a typical colony of this species on the Yellowstone near Yancey's but did not secure any.

Mountain Deer-mouse (Peromyscus maniculatus artemisiae) Abundant everywhere.

Mountain Rat, Pack-rat or Wood-rat (Neotoma cinerea) Said to be found, but I saw none.

Redbacked Vole or Field-mouse (Evotomys gapperi galei) Not taken yet in the Park but found in all the surrounding country, therefore, probable.

Common Field-mouse (Microtus pennsylvannicus modestus) Recorded by Vernon Bailey from Lower Geyser Basin in the Park.

Long-tailed Vole (Microtus mordax) Vernon Bailey records this from various surrounding localities, also from Tower Falls. Doubtless it is generally distributed. This is the bobtailed, short-eared, dark gray mouse that is found making runs in the thick grass, especially in low places.

Big-footed Vole (Microtus richardsoni macropus) Not yet taken in the Park, but found in surrounding mountains, therefore probable.

Muskrat (Fiber zibethicus osoyoosensis) Common and of general distribution.

Mole-gopher or Gray Gopher (Thomomys talpoides) A Gopher of some kind abounds in the Park. I assume it to be this.

Rocky Mt. Jumping Mouse (Zapus princeps) Found in all the surrounding country, and recorded by E. A. Preble from near Yellowstone Lake.

Yellow-haired Porcupine (Erethizon epixanthus) Somewhat common in the pine woods on the Continental Divide.

Coney, Rock Rabbit, Pika, or Calling Hare (Ochotona princeps) Abundant in all slide rock.

Rocky Mt. Cottontail (Sylvilagus nuttalli grangeri) Plentiful about Gardiner and in some of the lower regions of the Park, but not general.

Snowshoe Rabbit (Lepus bairdi) Common and generally distributed.

White-tailed Jack Rabbit (Lepus campestris) Common and generally distributed.

Mountain Lion, Cougar or Puma (Felis hippolestes) In 1897 it was considered extremely rare; probably not more than a dozen were then living in the Park; since then it seems to have increased greatly and is now somewhat common in the mountainous parts. Their numbers are given officially at 100 in 1912.

Canada Lynx (Lynx canadensis) Common.

Bobcat or Mountain-cat (Lynx uinta) Somewhat common.

The Big-tailed Fox (Vulpes macrourus) Common.

Timber Wolf (Canis occidentalis) Very rare, noticed only at Hell Roaring Creek and Slough Creek. On August 25, 1912, Lieut. M. Murray saw two in a meadow two miles southeast of Snow Shoe Cabin on Slough Creek. They were plainly seen in broad daylight; and were nearly white.

Coyote (Canis latrans) Abundant everywhere, although officially reckoned they numbered only 400 in 1912.

Otter (Lutra canadensis) Common, particularly around the Lake and the Canyon.

Mink (Lutreola vison energumenos) Common.

Long-tailed Weasel (Putorius longicauda) Said to be found. I did not see any.

Short-tailed Weasel (Putorius cicognanii) Included because its range includes the Park.

Marten (Mustela caurina) Found throughout the Park, but not common.

Pekan or Fisher (Mustela pennanti) Rare. Gen. G. S. Anderson tells me that in the early '90's he took the skin of one from a poacher.

Wolverine (Gulo luscus) Of general distribution, but not common.

Northern Skunk (Mephitis hudsonica) Rare, but found at Mammoth Hot Springs and Yancey's.

Badger (Taxidea taxus) Common.

Raccoon or Coon (Procyon lotor) Said to occur. Fifteen years ago at Gardiner I was shown one that was said to have been taken in the Park, but it was not certain.

Grizzly Bear (Ursus horribilis) Common. The official count gives 50 in 1912.

Blackbear (Ursus americanus) Abundant and increasing. The official count gives 100 in 1912.

Common or Masked Shrew (Sorex personatus) Never taken, but included because its known range surrounds the Park.

Marsh Shrew or Water Shrew (Neosorex palustris) Probably occurs there, since its known range surrounds the Park.

Long-eared Bat (Corynorhinus macrotis pallescens) A few were seen in the Devil's Kitchen, Mammoth Hot Springs, and one sent to the Biological Survey for identification. This is the only Bat taken, but the following are likely to be found, as their known range surrounds the Park:

Little Brown Bat (Myotis lucifugus) Silver-haired Bat (Lasionycteris noctivagans) Big Brown Bat (Eptesicus fuscus) Great Hoary Bat (Nycteris cinereus)

* * * * *

Transcriber's Notes

Bold text is indicated by equal symbols: =text=.

Italic text is indicated by underscores: text.

Moved some illustrations from their original positions to avoid breaking up paragraphs of text. The List of Half-tone Plates displays the original page numbers. Some apparently missing plates may have been edited out of the original version.

Corrected minor punctuation errors.

Page 61: Clomb could be a typo for climb: (rush as they might and did, and bounded and clomb,)

Page 123: Changed pased to passed: (men had passed near)

Page 155: Changed Bitteroot to Bitterroot: (This took place in the Bitterroot Mountains)

Page 157: Added missing exclamation point: (I heard the dreaded cry, "Yellow-Jackets!")

Page 165: Changed conspicious to conspicuous: (might otherwise make it too conspicuous.)

Page 176: Changed inclinded to inclined: (travellers will be inclined to bunch them)

Page 196: Changed go to to: (We went quietly to the edge of the timber)

Page 210: Plate XL was not included in the original book. (The picture, such as it is, I give as Plate XL, c.)

Page 213: Manoeuvring had an oe ligature in the original book: (it stood, and there was some pretty manoeuvring,)

Ernest Thompson Seton

Born

August 14, 1860
South Shields, England, United Kingdom

Died
October 23, 1946 (aged 86)
Seton Village, New Mexico, United States

Other names
"Ernest Evan Thompson", "Ernest Seton Thompson", "Black Wolf", "Chief"

Occupation
author, wildlife artist

Known for
founder of the Woodcraft Indians and founding pioneer of the Boy Scouts of America

Awards
John Burroughs Medal (1927)
Daniel Giraud Elliot Medal (1928)
Silver Buffalo Award

Ernest Thompson Seton (August 14, 1860 – October 23, 1946) was an author (published in the United Kingdom, Canada, and the US), wildlife artist, founder of the Woodcraft Indians, and one of the founding pioneers of the Boy Scouts of America (BSA). Seton also influenced Lord Baden-Powell, the founder of Scouting. His notable books related to Scouting include The Birch Bark Roll and The Boy Scout Handbook. He is responsible for the appropriation and incorporation of what he believed to be American Indian elements into the traditions of the BSA.

Early life

Ernest Thompson Seton, born Ernest Evan Thompson[1] in South Shields, County Durham (now part of South Tyneside, Tyne and Wear), England of Scottish parents, Seton's family emigrated to Canada in 1866. Most of his childhood was spent in Toronto. As a youth, he retreated to the woods to draw and study animals as a way of avoiding his abusive father. He won a scholarship in art to the Royal Academy in London, England.[2]

On his twenty-first birthday, Seton's father presented him with a bill for all the expenses connected with his childhood and youth, including the fee charged by the doctor who delivered him. He paid the bill, but never spoke to his father again.[3][4]

Ernest changed his name to Ernest Thompson Seton, believing that Seton had been an important family name. He became successful as a writer, artist and naturalist, and moved to New York City to further his career. Seton later lived at Wyndygoul, an estate that he built in Cos Cob, a section of Greenwich, Connecticut. After experiencing vandalism by the local youth, Seton invited them to his estate for a weekend where he told them what he claimed were stories of the American Indians and of nature.[5]

He formed the Woodcraft Indians in 1902 and invited the local youth to join. Despite the name, the group was made up of non-native boys and girls. The stories became a series of articles written for the Ladies Home Journal, and were eventually collected in The Birch Bark Roll of the Woodcraft Indians in 1906.

Scouting

Seton met Scouting's founder, Lord Baden-Powell, in 1906. Baden-Powell had read Seton's book, The Birch Bark Roll of the Woodcraft Indians, and was greatly intrigued by it. The pair met and shared ideas. Baden-Powell went on to found the Scouting movement worldwide, and Seton became the president of the committee that founded the Boy Scouts of America (BSA) and was its first (and only) Chief Scout. The position of Chief Scout was removed, and the position "Chief Scout Executive" was taken on by James West. His Woodcraft Indians (a youth organization), combined with the early attempts at Scouting from the YMCA and other organizations, and Daniel Carter Beard's Sons of Daniel Boone, to form the BSA.[6] The work of Seton and Beard is in large part the basis of the Traditional Scouting movement.[7]

Seton was Chief Scout of the BSA from 1910–1915 and his work is in large part responsible for the appropriation and incorporation of what he believed to be American Indian elements into the traditions of the BSA. However, he had significant personality and philosophical clashes with Beard and James E. West.

In addition to disputes about the content of Seton's contributions to the Boy Scout Handbook, conflicts also arose about the suffrage activities of his wife, Grace Gallatin Seton Thompson, and his British citizenship. The citizenship issue arose partly because of his high position within BSA, and the federal charter West was attempting to obtain for the BSA required its board members to be United States citizens. Seton drafted his written resignation on January 29, 1915, but he did not send it to BSA until May.[8]

Personal life

Seton married twice. His first marriage was to Grace Gallatin in 1896. Their only daughter, Ann, was born in 1904 and died in 1990. Ann, who later changed her first name, became a best-selling author of historical and biographical novels as Anya Seton. According to Ann's introduction to the novel Green Darkness, Grace was a practicing Theosophist. Ernest and Grace divorced in 1935, and Ernest soon married Julia M. Buttree. Julia would write works by herself and with Ernest. They did not have any biological children, but did adopt an infant daughter, Beulah (Dee) Seton (later Dee Seton Barber), in 1938. Dee Seton Barber, a talented embroiderer of articles for synagogues such as Torah mantles, died in 2006.

Writing and later life

Seton was an early pioneer of the modern school of animal fiction writing, his most popular work being Wild Animals I Have Known (1898), which contains the story of his killing of the wolf Lobo. He later became involved in a literary debate known as the nature fakers controversy, after John Burroughs published an article in 1903 in the Atlantic Monthly attacking writers of sentimental animal stories. The controversy lasted for four years and included important American environmental and political figures of the day, including President Theodore Roosevelt.[9]

In 1907, Seton and the naturalist Edward Alexander Preble verified a claim from ten years earlier by the frontiersman Charles "Buffalo" Jones that Jones and his hunting party of musk oxen had shot and fended off a hungry wolf pack near the Great Slave Lake in Canada. Seton and Preble discovered the remains of the animals near Jones's long abandoned cabin.[10]

For his work, Lives of Game Animals, Volume 4, Seton was awarded the Daniel Giraud Elliot Medal from the National Academy of Sciences in 1928 .[11] In 1931, he became a United States citizen. Seton was associated with the Santa Fe arts and literary community during the mid-1930s and early 1940s, which comprised a group of artists and authors including author and artist Alfred Morang, sculptor and potter Clem Hull, painter Georgia O'Keeffe, painter Randall Davey, painter Raymond Jonson, leader of the Transcendental Painters Group, and artist Eliseo Rodriguez.[12] He was made a member of the Royal Canadian Academy of Arts.[13]

He died in Seton Village in northern New Mexico at the age of eighty-six. Seton was cremated in Albuquerque. In 1960, in honor of his 100th birthday and the 350th anniversary of Santa Fe, his daughter Dee and his grandson, Seton Cottier (son of Anya), scattered the ashes over Seton Village from an airplane.[14]

Legacy

The Philmont Scout Ranch houses the Seton Memorial Library and Museum. Seton Castle in Santa Fe, built by Seton as his last residence, housed many of his other items. Seton Castle burned down in 2005; fortunately all the artwork, manuscripts, books, etc., had been removed to storage before renovation was to have begun.[15]

The Academy for the Love of Learning, an educational organization in Santa Fe, acquired Seton Castle and its contents in 2003. The new Academy Center opened in 2011 includes a gallery and archives featuring artwork and other materials as part of its Seton Legacy Project. The Seton Legacy Project organized a major exhibition on Seton opening at the New Mexico History Museum on May 23, 2010, the catalog published as Ernest Thompson Seton: The Life and Legacy of an Artist and Conservationist by David L. Witt.

Roger Tory Peterson drew inspiration for his field guide from the simple diagram of ducks that Seton included in Two Little Savages.[16]

Several of Seton's works are written from the perspective of a predator and were an influence upon Robert T. Bakker's Raptor Red.[17]

Seton is honoured by the Ernest Thompson Seton Scout Reservation in Greenwich, Connecticut, USA, and with the E.T. Seton Park in Toronto, Canada. Obtained in the early 1960s as the site of future Metro Toronto Zoo, the land was later used to establish parkland and home to the Ontario Science Centre. Seton is mentioned in Philip Roth's Novel, "Nemesis," where he is credited for having introduced Indian Lore to the American Camping movement.[18]